D1602368

In the Shadow of Frémont

Edward Meyer Kern. Daguerreotype. Huntington Library.

IN THE SHADOW OF FRÉMONT

Edward Kern and the Art of Exploration, 1845-1860

Second Edition

by
Robert V. Hine

University of Oklahoma Press : Norman

By ROBERT V. HINE

California's Utopian Colonies (San Marino, Calif., 1953; New Haven, Conn., 1966; New York, 1973)

(editor) *William Andrew Spalding, Los Angeles Newspaperman: An Autobiographical Account* (San Marino, Calif., 1961)

Edward Kern and American Expansion (New Haven, Conn., 1962)

(editor) *The Irvine Ranch,* by Robert Glass Cleland (San Marino, Calif., 1962)

Bartlett's West: Drawing the Mexican Boundary (New Haven, Conn., 1968)

(editor) *Soldier in the West: Letters of Theodore Talbot During His Services in California, Mexico, and Oregon, 1845-53* (with Savoie Lottinville; Norman, 1972)

(editor) *The American Frontier: Readings and Documents* (with Edwin R. Bingham; Boston, 1972)

The American West: An Interpretive History (Boston, 1973)

Community on the American Frontier: Separate but Not Alone (Norman, 1980)

California Utopianism: Contemplations of Eden (San Francisco, 1981)

In the Shadow of Frémont: Edward Kern and the Art of Exploration, 1845-1860 (second edition of *Edward Kern and American Expansion;* Norman, 1982)

Library of Congress Cataloging in Publication Data

Hine, Robert V., 1921–
   In the shadow of Frémont.

   Previously published as: Edward Kern and American expansion.
   Bibliography: p. 163
   Includes index.
   1. Kern, Edward Meyer, 1823-1863. 2. West (U.S.)—Description and travel—To 1848. 3. West (U.S.)—Description and travel—1848-1860. 4. United States—Exploring expeditions. 5. Explorers—West (U.S.)—Biography. 6. West (U.S.) in art. I. Title.
F592.K4H5   1982   978'.02   82-40326
                        AACR2

Chapter decorations by Dale R. Roylance

Contents

Illustrations

Preface to the First Edition

The nineteenth century was a wandering time. It included the most enormous migrations of all history. From farms to cities, from Old World to New (and often back again), from east to west, from frontier to frontier, from known soils to enigmatic lands, men moved. And what more congenial place for a wanderer than the American West? These expanses were, it is true, to be peopled by men like John Marsh and Oliver Larkin and Brigham Young, essentially settlers at heart. But there was also an army of rovers who lived or had lived vagabond lives: John Sutter and Isaac Graham, Jedediah Smith and the Patties, Ewing Young and Joseph Walker, Sam Houston and Richard King, Nathaniel Wyeth and Benjamin Bonneville, Lewis Garrard and Josiah Gregg, James Marshall and Henry Comstock. These men, like John Smith and Daniel Boone, were the Childe Harolds of the New World. John Charles Frémont was such a pilgrim, though a scientific one, and so were his assistants, the brothers Edward, Richard, and Benjamin Kern.

There were economic reasons for the restlessness, but for the Kerns as for the century the fever was the result of a contagious Romanticism. Their sketches in the field may have been realistic and topographic, but, with a flute and poetry in their knapsack, the brothers' lives were pure Byron. "Who cares for the artificial world across the continent, when he can thus enjoy wild and uncontrolled independence?" asked Joseph Revere, one of Edward's friends, and it could have been a Kern talking.

The Romantic impulse, inasmuch as it was nomadic and undisciplined and exalted imaginative and intuitive knowledge above the empirical, may seem to conflict with science. But if this conflict existed and was to have the profound implications that Joseph Wood Krutch portrayed in *The Modern Temper* three-quarters of a century later, it was not evident to the Kerns. Their lives moved easily between art and the topographical and natural sciences. Their concern for accuracy and precision encompassed both their art and their science. Their wanderlust was a part of the exploratory adventure of science, and their travels created a stream of raw data pouring into the laboratories and academies of the East.

Edward ("Ned") Kern was fifteen years old when the United States Army in 1838 separated the Topographic Corps from the Engineers, thus setting in motion the administrative machinery for the peculiar task of drafting the first maps and concrete images of the trans-Mississippi West. Through the Topographic Corps Kern made his chief contribution as a scientist. When, a quarter of a century later, the corps ceased its separate existence, Kern's scientific career had moved to other channels; but it is curiously symbolic that the Topographic Corps was dissolved in the same year that Ned Kern died.

Ned was the most important of the Kern brothers for this study because he initiated their wanderings, eventually persuaded his two brothers to join him with Frémont, and lived through a lifetime of adventures to die in bed. Both Ben and Dick were murdered in the course of work which, if completed, might have placed them as prominently in history as Ned; but as the game was played, the first and last cards fell to the youngest of the three. His, too, was the deepest involvement with Frémont, because he alone of the brothers had felt an attachment approaching discipleship. Ned's early respect for Frémont was strong enough to be revived after a period of withering hatred and to emerge like an underground stream when the two were finally brought together again.

In the last ten years of Ned's life he dealt not with the continental West, but rather with seas and coastlines. Nevertheless, his work for Navy officers like John Rodgers and John Brooke was in substance the same as for Army men like Frémont—drawing the figure and charting the route for the political and commercial growth of his country. The life of Kern was a camera lucida of American expansion, as that expansion is described by Richard Van Alstyne: "global in its reach . . . of multiple thrusts, seaward as well as landward."

I have enjoyed knowing Edward Kern and his brothers. I would have liked them as friends. They philosophized little, and that perhaps is unfortunate; but they faced life and the unknown with enthusiasm. They echoed Wordsworth: "Bliss was it in that dawn to be alive." Their periods of gloom and depression, even accompanying hardship and death, were short. They were not ambitious, like Frémont; their drive seemed to stem from an inner need, a curiosity which sought satisfaction for its own sake. Their sense of humor saved them from extending their zeal to personal aggrandizement. Flattery they would neither give nor accept. Hypocrisy they would not tolerate. Frémont, the dedicated searcher of the untraced, they would worship; Frémont, the accuser of others to shield himself, they would hate. They had humor, vitality, reserve, generosity, loyalty to family and friends, and, above all, a respect for knowledge.

The opportunity of knowing these men and writing of

them has placed me in debt to many. The financial assistance of the Guggenheim Foundation, the Haynes Foundation, and the Research Committee of the University of California, Riverside, has been most generous. The staffs of the following institutions have given inestimable help: the Huntington Library; the Yale University Library; the Library of Congress; the National Archives; the Boston Museum of Fine Arts; the Gray Herbarium, Harvard University; the John Carter Brown Library, Providence; the Library of the Museum of New Mexico, Santa Fe; the Newberry Library, Chicago; the Gilcrease Foundation, Tulsa; the Museum of the Naval Academy, Annapolis; the Scripps College Library; the Bancroft Library, Berkeley; and the Libraries of the University of California at Riverside and Los Angeles. The *Utah Historical Quarterly* has given permission to reproduce a few passages which originally appeared in that magazine.

The number of individuals to whom I am obligated is legion; the following list is a partial expression of gratitude. My colleagues Mack E. Thompson, Ernst Ekman, and L. Marshall Van Deusen; as well as John Hawgood, University of Birmingham, England, for helpfully criticizing portions of the manuscript; Leslie Bliss, Robert Wark, Miss Mary Isabel Fry, and Miss Haydée Noya, among many others, of the Huntington Library; J. S. Holliday and Mrs. Julia Macleod of the Bancroft Library; Lawrence Clark Powell and Maurice Block of the University of California, Los Angeles; Henry P. Rossiter, Miss Helen Willard, and Mrs. Anne Freedburg of the Boston Museum of Fine Arts; David DeHarport and Mrs. Katherine B. Edsall of the Peabody Museum of Archaeology and Ethnology, Harvard University; Thomas M. Beggs and Herbert Friedman of the Smithsonian Institution; Mrs. Venia T. Phillips of the Philadelphia Academy of Natural Sciences; George M. Brooke, Jr., Virginia Military Institute; Mrs. John M. Wolfe and Mrs. James F. McGarry, Jr., Merion, Pennsylvania; Mrs. Raoul

L. Drapeau, Chelmsford, Massachusetts; Erwin G. Gudde and Mrs. Spencer C. Browne, Berkeley; Fred Rosenstock, Denver; Roger Butterfield, *Life* Magazine; the Reverend Frederick Bohme, Church Divinity School of the Pacific, Berkeley; Thomas Leavitt of the Pasadena Art Museum; Beaumont Newhall, Eastman House, Rochester; Mrs. Clyde Porter, Kansas City; Justin Turner, Los Angeles; James W. Arrott, Sapello, New Mexico; Mrs. Olivia M. W. Kollock, La Jolla, California.

At every stage my wife has read the manuscript for me and shared each problem.

Perhaps I might thank all of the above by using the words of Edward Kern, standing on the threshold of the West in 1845, "Blicke zum Himmel."

R. V. H.

University of California, Riverside
April, 1961

Preface to the Second Edition

"Our central calling, our main task on this planet, is the heroic," wrote the fiery young anthropologist Ernest Becker in 1973.[1] Like morality, however, the heroic life is not easily attainable. To achieve it, we must wrest from a cynical society the opportunity for great deeds and conjure within our doubting selves the images of new worlds. Ultimately we must face death without qualms. To accomplish these ends, we must build a screen against the agony and panic at the core of existence. The screen represses and compromises reality and hence is an illusion. Because it lightens the burden of dread, it offers time for generosity, courage, and, most important, creativity. The creative hero is free to make a statement for others and is brave enough to say something anew. Heroism, as Becker said, rests upon this creative illusion, and the idea is aptly demonstrated in the life of Edward Kern.

Kern's days were certainly creative, graced as they were with pencil and brush, collector's bottles, and scientific instruments. The man was both artistic and artful, aesthetic and adroit. The artfulness trimmed the aesthetic to

[1] *The Denial of Death* (New York, 1973).

fit a practical goal, the exploration of a young nation's potential resources. And appropriately so: youth for both men and nations is a time for testing, whether of muscle or of purpose. Thus creativity for such times expresses the excitement of confrontation and seldom dwells on retreat or bitterness.

Perhaps Kern's transcendence of bitterness was a clue to his corresponding illusion. Art for him, like life, was bathed in a quiet innocence. How could he address the implications of his explorations without assessing the causes of the rise and fall of national power? His illusion lay in the assumption that whatever his art and science portrayed could lead only to growth and honor, never to decline or disrepute. The art of heroes does not stare long into the eyes of death. Heroic art must remain partly blind.

Edward Kern seemed unaware of the industrial threshold on which his nation stood and toward which so many of his activities moved. Did his heroism require an avoidance of the consequences of his acts? Modern scholarship, particularly that of the twenty years since this book was first published, has stripped us of such illusions. William Goetzmann's Pulitzer Prize work on Western exploration showed men like Kern as the tools of hard-knuckled imperialists. Modernization theorists like Walter Rostow went beyond the commercial appropriation of mineral resources (including Pacific guano) to describe the resulting social fragmentation of once stable communities. Minority historians exposed the racial condescension toward Indians and Orientals masked in the explorations of Kern and his counterparts. What is left for the heroic?

A great deal. Personally Kern struggled successfully against disease and despair but, unlike Melville's Ahab, never raised the possibility that such agonies might lie at the heart of the matter. In the same way he neither saw nor understood the possibilities of national guilt and responsibility. His philosophy left him free to earn high marks in art and science, the rewards of his brush, the fruits of his maps and charts. The art of his exploration thus prefigured his heroism, the grand but myopic central calling of men like Edward Kern.

My thanks for help with the second edition go especially to David Weber, of Southern Methodist University; Ronald Tyler, of the Amon Carter Museum; Peter Hassrick, of the Buffalo Bill Historical Center; and Patricia Trenton, of the Palm Springs Desert Museum.

R. V. H.

Riverside, California
February, 1982

In the Shadow of Frémont

CHAPTER 1

Westport

The Louisiana Purchase has been considered by men like
Henry Adams and Bernard de Voto to be one of the most
important events in modern history because it turned the
American nation irrevocably westward. Though the direction thereafter remained clear, the nature of the destination
was long a mystery. The traditional, familiar westward pull,
from the time of John Eliot's missionary drive to Henry
Thoreau's natural inclination, had kept most Americans so
aware of their West that to describe a Mohawk Indian or
the Ohio River was as easy as calling up a vision of home.
But for the land beyond the Ohio and Mississippi there
were no such images, no pictures, and the inevitable temp-
tation was either to read Mohawk Indians and Ohio rivers
into the blank spaces or to evoke a vague fancy. Within a
decade, Lewis and Clark and Zebulon Pike made prose
efforts to describe the new country, but, as de Voto has
said, Americans acted on these printed words "to create a
multiform and fantastic West." For an unclouded view of

their Canaan, they needed more than bits of prose: "somehow images must be formed for their avid eyes."[1]

The demand for such images was partially met in the 1830's when George Catlin and Karl Bodmer brought from beyond the Mississippi drawings which proved that Mandans were hardly Mohawks and that the castellated landscapes along the Missouri were unlike anything the Ohio ever watered. Following them in the 1840's a headstrong, intense, but soft-spoken lieutenant of the United States Topographical Corps, John Charles Frémont, four times rode west from the Mississippi. On each trip he included in his train an artist to translate the new country into a visual image. The controversies that later swirled about Frémont—in the conquest of California, in the campaign for the presidency, in the contretemps with Lincoln —obscured the fact that his finest contributions lay in shaping an early picture of the West.

In this work one of his chief aides was a painter from Philadelphia, Edward Meyer Kern, a virile hotspur with a temperament matching his deep red hair and a spirit stirred by curiosity and driven by Romantic restlessness. Curiosity was perhaps a natural part of his artistic equipment, but Kern also suffered from a desire for that lonely exaltation of the ego which comes from being the first man on a scene, for the zest of being able to say of a day's march that no white foot has preceded mine.

Ned Kern (for Ned was what most men called him) was tall and thin with a long face accentuated by moustache and spade beard. His hair was red, so dark that many called it black, and it surrounded his ears in curls. The curls must have been natural, for he was not a dandy, and his brother once sent him a comb in the hope that Ned would bring himself to use it. He was gregarious, a member of the Odd Fellows Lodge, given to banter and joke. Yet at the same

1. *Across the Wide Missouri* (Boston, 1947), p. 395.

time he was proud and maintained a certain dignity in his humor. Behind his gray eyes lay an intuitive sense of color; his journals were sprinkled with insights into "bluish tints" and "brighter greens." And through these colors he saw a Nature which was soft and benign. Like a true Romantic, he worshiped Nature; and there may have moved deep within him a strain of Romantic melancholy, for his one surviving likeness in daguerreotype suggests around his eyes a feeling of sadness.

His star was to lead him to the West,[2] yet he was no Hawkeye, no Deerslayer; James Fenimore Cooper might have described him as "a single gentleman under the influence of the winds."[3] His family was genteel; he was better acquainted with Chippendale and silver than with a stone stool or a tin cup. The son of a custom-house collector for the port of Philadelphia, Ned's background implied none of the rootlessness of a frontier. During the Revolution, for example, his grandmother had stood firm against the Hessians in her cabbage patch, and her descendants had held the same house for generations.

Edward's father had died in 1842 and his mother the following year, leaving eight children—the youngest, Edward, then twenty; the eldest, Mary, thirty-eight. The elder Kerns had seen that their children were well educated. One of the boys, Benjamin, earned an M.D. at the Pennsylvania Medical College. He and the others wrote well, read widely, and attended the theater. Three of the boys—John, Jr., Richard, and Edward—had established themselves as artists and teachers of drawing. When he was only eighteen, Edward had illustrated a poem of Robert Burns in his sister's memory album and proved he was already a competent colorist. *(Fig. 5)* Edward and Richard had even succeeded

2. The Burlington (Iowa) *Hawk-Eye*, May 3, 1849, said that two of the three Kern brothers (Benjamin, Richard, or Edward) "kept school" in Burlington during that city's "younger days."

3. *Last of the Mohicans*, Introduction.

in showing works at the Artists' Fund Society in 1840 and
1841—Edward, a water-color snow scene; Richard, oils of
"Muckross Abbey" and "Swedes' Church, Wilmington, Delaware."[4]

The artistic achievement of the three boys need not have
resulted from formal teaching; it more probably developed
from within the confines of the family and from self-instruction. Once John, the elder, had become a teacher, Edward
and Richard must have absorbed much from him. But even
without John, self-instruction was a common phenomenon
of the day. There were countless manuals. "Anyone who can
learn to write can learn to draw," began Chapman's *American Drawing Book* a few years later.[5] In such guides Edward
could have learned all his techniques—the complications
of spherical perspective, the elements of composition, even
how to sharpen a pencil.

By whatever means, he had learned well. By the time he
left Philadelphia he was deft at water-color tinting, and in
general his work argued a competent understanding of
color, of shadow, of pencil and brush technique. He knew
the accepted devices for concentrating attention or suggest-
ing depth through grouping and spacing. And he height-
ened his sketches with white in a way that showed awareness
of a long tradition extending back at least to Dürer.

4. The basic source for Kern family background is Helen Wolfe, "Some
Kern Notes Written for Members of the Family from Data Collected over a
Period of Years" (typescript, Huntington and Bancroft libraries). For art
details see George C. Groce and David H. Wallace, *Dictionary of Artists
in America, 1564–1860*, New Haven, 1957, and Anna Wells Rutledge, ed.,
Cumulative Record of Exhibition Catalogues, Philadelphia, 1955.

5. John G. Chapman, *American Drawing Book: A Manual for the Amateur*, New York, 1947. The Pennsylvania Academy of the Fine Arts has no
record of enrollment for any of the Kerns, and the Artists' Fund Society
is no longer extant. Edward and Richard dreamed of studying in Europe,
but their hopes were never fulfilled. A contemporary Philadelphia artist
whose life pattern was similar to the Kerns, in that he was largely self-
taught, was James Hamilton, who, interestingly enough, later helped
Frémont illustrate his *Memoirs* and very possibly at that time worked up
some of Edward's California drawings posthumously for the engraver.

Philadelphia was a center of the arts. Between 1838 and 1845, when Edward left for the West, thirty-eight paintings of Thomas Birch, thirty-two of Thomas Doughty, thirty-four of James Hamilton, twenty-seven of Henry Inman, and no fewer than seventy-four of Thomas Sully appeared in Philadelphia exhibitions, along with smaller numbers of Thomas Cole, Jasper Cropsey, James Lambdin, and Emanuel Leutze.[6] The Kerns knew personally many of the younger artists, and tramping through the galleries could substitute for considerable institutional training. By communing with the works of Thomas Cole or Thomas Birch, Ned Kern soaked up the mood of the Hudson River School; he could learn portraiture by studying canvases by Thomas Sully; and if he wandered into one of George Catlin's or John Mix Stanley's forests of Indian drawings, he had indelibly impressed on him techniques for interpreting the West.

But looking at art and making a living were two different things. One house provided a studio for the painting and teaching of the three artist-brothers, in addition to medical offices for Ben. The income for the youngest of three art teachers in the same studio must have been meager, and this fact might very well have prodded Edward's curiosity about the West. With Frémont he could explore the Western mystery and return with money in his pocket.

There was one other factor which, although we have no direct evidence of the fact, may have been crucial in Kern's desire to go West: his health. Ned was an epileptic, which may explain his thinness and the sadness in his eyes. Although there would have been little hope that the West could effect a cure, it might provide a cloak for his seizures,

6. According to Helen Wolfe, Edward Kern's grandniece, Emanuel Leutze used a photograph of Edward as a model for the central figure in his mural "Westward the Course of Empire Takes Its Way," on the west staircase of the national Capitol; see her "Some Kern Notes," Huntington Library.

when they came. No strangers with prying eyes, only the sympathetic hands of a few comrades on the trail, the anonymity of open space—these may have appealed to an epileptic.[7]

Ned was not alone in his wish to go West. If Frémont had wanted thousands of men, said the *Missouri Reporter*, he could have procured them easily. Crowds anxious to accompany him gathered wherever he went. There had been forty-two applicants for the position of artist alone.[8] Most of them had read Frémont's report of his first two expeditions, in which the "pathfinder" had emerged as a symbol of the trans-Mississippi West, a Galahad on horse or in rubber boat, jousting with the unknown. Thereby the West entered a thousand parlors; and even those who couldn't read might pore over the dramatic lithographs of Charles Preuss—Indian tepees by Fort Laramie, the white, glacial bulk of Pike's Peak, the teeth of the Wind River peaks above spruce trees, Gothic columns along the Columbia. The art work had been most effective, and Frémont would have preferred to take Preuss as artist again, but he could not reckon with Preuss' wife. She had worried enough

7. Evidence for Edward Kern's epilepsy is from three sources: his Philadelphia death certificate, in which the cause of death reads "epileptic convulsions"; an entry in John Brooke, Journal, November 6, 1859: "This morning Mr. Kern had one of those attacks of an epileptic character to which he is subject at intervals of four or five months"; and John Brooke to John Rogers, June 1, 1865, Naval Foundation Papers, Library of Congress. Brooke knew Kern fairly closely from about 1853 to 1860. Admittedly it is not wholly safe to generalize from this evidence a lifetime of epilepsy; conceivably the disease might not have developed until the late 1850's. But placed beside Edward's frequent illnesses of a rather mysterious character in California and New Mexico (see below, pp. 32–33, 46, 85), the grounds seem strong enough.

8. *Missouri Reporter*, June 7, 1845, as quoted in folder 10, Dale Morgan Collection, Huntington Library. Theodore Talbot to his mother, May 30, 1845, Talbot Papers, Library of Congress. Unless otherwise noted, all the quotations from Talbot in this chapter are from May–July 1845, letters in the Talbot Papers, Library of Congress. For the number of artist-applicants see R. Kern to J. R. Bartlett, March 14, 1851, Fort Sutter Papers, Huntington Library.

about her husband and wanted no more of it. So Preuss remained behind, watching the Potomac from his Washington house and smoking his pipe in the arbor, while others moved on to sketch wilder rivers.

Ned Kern had read that report, and it had transformed his life. He was twenty-two years old, his curiosity was at its height, and like a later artist who asked for a similar job, he idolized Frémont as "the beau ideal of all that was chivalrous and noble."[9]

If he wanted the job there was politicking to be done. His best hopes lay with a fellow artist from Philadelphia, Joseph Drayton, who was then busy in Washington cataloguing drawings and specimens which he had brought back from the Wilkes Pacific Expedition three years earlier. Drayton spoke with Lieutenant Henry Eld, a colleague from the Wilkes venture, and together they approached Frémont about Kern. At the same time Edward sent Frémont some sample sketches, including some botanical drawings, which pleased the captain considerably. In March 1845 Ned wrote his friends in Washington grateful thanks. He had been promised the appointment.

Frémont warned Kern that his duties would be arduous. He was to receive, however, not only three dollars a day in wages beginning May 1, 1845, but ten cents a mile traveling expenses to the rendezvous in Missouri. The job had materialized on terms as handsome as Ned could have wished.[10]

So with an abundant curiosity and an unknown West for its object, Ned Kern set forth in 1845. He traveled down the Ohio River with his doctor brother, Ben, who accompanied him, perhaps, to avert the danger of Ned having an epileptic attack among strangers. In St. Louis the two part-

9. Solomon N. Carvalho, *Incidents of Travel and Adventure in the Far West* (New York, 1856), p. 18.

10. John Charles Frémont to Edward Kern, May 1, 1845, Huntington Library; J. C. Frémont to [Torrey?], March 22, 1845, Southwest Museum.

ed, and Ned with Frémont himself and a group of his men
boarded the *Henry Bry* bound for Westport, in what is now
Kansas City. On the steamer as it paddled and churned up
the Missouri, the men, bored by the confines of a side-
wheeler, indolently watched the creeping banks, damned
the towheads which rose like whales in their path, drank,
smoked, sang, played cards—anything to absorb time. But
Ned could more contentedly settle his lanky six-foot body
on the deck's edge, pull out his pad, and draw, rather than
damn, the river. His job had begun. Beyond the Missouri
lay the plains and mountains, the animals, fish, and birds—
the stuff of the American West.

With letting of steam and ringing of bells, the boat
docked at Kansas Landing, like Westport a part of modern
Kansas City. The morning, June 9, 1845, was cold and
drizzling. The baggage was hustled ashore. Kern and his
friends built fires, cooked a quick breakfast, and sat about
on bales and duffel bags of private belongings (called "possible sacks") waiting for orders. Before noon the wagons
arrived from camp and carried off the great packets and
hogsheads of flour and bacon, coffee and sugar, instruments
and iron pickets. Most of the men, trudging behind the
wagons, were sidetracked by the *aguardiente* of a local sa-
loon, and eventually arrived in camp, yelling "Ole Dan
Tucker's come to town" and breaking into the popular
song "Lucy Neale" from a recent Philadelphia minstrel
show:

> Miss Lucy she was taken sick,
> She eat too much corn meal,
> The Doctor he did gib her up,
> Alas! poor Lucy Neale.

Meanwhile Kern followed on horse with the captain's party,
clomping past the handful of houses in Kansas Landing and
over three or four miles of rolling, timbered country to the
village of Westport.

Two of the men riding beside Kern were applicants for positions as artists of the expedition—swaggering Alfred S. Waugh and his friend John B. Tisdale. Waugh had wandered west and was in New Orleans when he and Tisdale, another foot-loose artist, had read of Frémont's plans. Hurrying up the river to St. Louis, they had found the captain and introduced themselves. Frémont had been noncommittal about the job, uncertain of their qualifications, and not at all sure he could afford more than one artist. Like dozens of other eager applicants, Waugh and Tisdale trooped along to the outfitting camp. Ned loaned them money for expenses.

Westport, though it had not reached the importance of Independence, had in its twelve boisterous years grown into a major launching center. From there Frémont had embarked on both of his previous expeditions. Similar parties bound for either the Santa Fe Trail or the Oregon Trail characteristically established temporary camps a few miles beyond Westport to assemble company and supplies. For the Santa Fe traveler the site was strategic because it saved fording the Kansas River. It held advantages over Independence because it was further west while still within range of steamboat transportation.

In the spring of 1845 the town experienced its annual turbulence. Traders haggled over mules; departing mountaineers had a final fling with liquor and women; Indian men, unsmiling, watched Indian girls catch the eyes of white admirers; Mexicans hired out as hostlers and muleteers; farmers drove carloads of produce to market. Ned Kern called it "a dirty place filled with Indians, Spaniards, Jews and all sorts and sizes of folk." Into this tumult rode the artists and officers, and here they divided. Frémont and the lieutenants stayed overnight at the house of a local government agent; Kern and the others set off for camp.[11]

11. Charles H. Carey, ed., *The Journals of Theodore Talbot, 1843 and 1849–52* (Portland, Ore., 1931), p. 6.

Once out of town they looked over the open prairie, the long undulations accentuated by late-afternoon shadows, the deep grasses, the groves of ash and sycamore and pig-nut hickory in the stream-fed draws. Thunderheads in the far west intensified the immensity of the horizons. Kern now joined that large group of men who viewed this prairie in the 1840's and never forgot it. They entered in their journals the most glowing descriptions, word pictures of "the emerald swells" and the "great green ocean of the prairies." Even hardheaded traders like Josiah Gregg often succumbed: "These gay meadows wear their most fanciful piebald robes from the earliest spring till divested of them by the hoary frosts of autumn." There were dozens of rococo descriptions, travelers "luxuriating in the blooming wilderness of sweets," watching the heavens and earth meet "on one vast carpet of green," while after a rain "the laughing flowerets, newly invigorated from the nectarine draught, seemed to vie with each other in the exhalation of their sweetest odors. The blushing strawberry, scarce yet divested of its rich burden of fruit, kissed my every step." The fields stretched full of flowers: the wild tea and spotted tulip, the pink spider wort, the indigo and larkspur. And the groves along the streams were choked with fruit: grapes just forming, wild plums, red and black currants, persimmons still green, and gooseberries.[12]

The three riders, artistic feelings alive, were thoroughly captivated. On reaching the crest of a small hill, they looked down upon the Frémont camp, "like some distant fleet of vessels at anchor on a heaving sea." The camp itself was on a slight rise surrounded by clumps of trees and close to a

12. The prairie descriptions are in the following order: Francis Parkman, *Journals*, ed. Mason Wade (2 vols. New York, 1947), 2, 421, 417; Josiah Gregg, *Commerce of the Prairies* (Norman, Okla., 1954), p. 363; Edwin Bryant, *What I Saw in California* (Santa Ana, Calif., 1936), p. 10; Alonzo Delano, *Across the Plains and among the Diggings* (New York, 1936), p. 4; Rufus Sage, *Scenes in the Rocky Mountains* (Philadelphia, 1846), p. 15.

spring which ran off in a small stream. Multitudes, hoping
like Waugh and Tisdale for a place on the roster, had converged on the campsite. The baggage from Kansas Landing
had arrived only a short time before, and there was confusion. But supper, cooking in big pots slung over the fires,
drew the band together. Before long Ned and his friends
were among the men, "cheerful hearts and willing spirits,"
talking loudly, laughing, and after supper joining in a few
songs.

That night Kern took blankets and spread a bed under
the body of a wagon. If he thought at all before sleep, he
might have imagined himself for the first time really in the
West. The border of the states ran only yards away. Beyond
lay the territories, and then Mexico. Those northern loosely
held provinces of Mexico were the targets of expansionist
senators led by Thomas Hart Benton, Frémont's father-in-
law, and the American push to the Pacific—in Mexican
eyes the march of a ravenous monster—would surely cause
trouble sooner or later. In the summer of 1845 the new
president, James Polk, still hoped to buy all of Upper California, but it was clear to most men that a Mexican refusal
to sell would only preface stronger methods. Hence an exploring expedition, scientific though it might be, recruited
sixty men, a rather large number for the purposes of either
science or protection from normal hazards. And the captain
offered sharpshooting prizes to keep his men alert. Each
man may not have been as well armed as in George Derby's
parody of such expeditions in his *Phoenixiana* ("with four
of Colt's revolvers, a Minie rifle, a copy of Col. Benton's
speech on the Pacific Railroad, and a mountain howitzer"),
but they did each have a percussion-lock Hawkin rifle and
two pistols, making a total of guns unusually large for an
expedition merely scientific.

That night there was a thunderstorm and a cataract of
rain. The morning was still stormy, but there was hot
coffee and bacon. Frémont, sitting small and delicately

well-bred in the saddle, rode into camp with his lieutenants. In spite of the weather the encampment further organized itself: a flag flew, a few white marquee tents were pitched, the men were arranged into ten messes of about seven each, and provisions and utensils were apportioned.

Frémont's own mess was small—only the captain himself, James McDowell (his wife's cousin), and Alexis Godey, faithful veteran of the second expedition. The second mess, to which Ned was assigned, included the two lieutenants, James W. Abert and William G. Peck; Henry King; Theodore Talbot; and the Indian boy, Chinook. As aides the six had a Negro servant, a German cook, and a French muleteer.

In the confusing, preparatory weeks when there were not enough tents to go around, Frémont directed the officers and artists to temporary lodging nearer town. Kern, with Waugh and Tisdale and the two lieutenants, found on the outskirts of Westport a room at the farm of Lindsey Lewis. If the Lewises were at first pleased with the extra income, a week later they may not have felt so, for their roomers were practical jokers and amused themselves by ringing a bell on top of the house at all hours of the day and night.

In the evenings they would sometimes sit outside, singing and joking, maybe telling the current story of the Missouri woman who asked a returning mountaineer if the *hos*tile Indians were as savage as those who fought on foot. They were young and loved a good tale, Kern as well as any. As Ned said, "We are a great set of punsters, at it all the time." A new acquaintance and future messmate, Theodore Talbot, a Frémont veteran, had two initial impressions of Ned—long legs and good humor. Talbot observed well, for Ned's wry humor was consistently evident. When Andrew Jackson died, Ned hoped he might find a "snug nook near the fire in heaven and not be compelled to join in the songs." Later, on a hard, dry march after an incident when the cook had accidentally boiled soap in the coffee,

Ned sardonically commented, "Rather unlucky just now, when coffee is coffee."[13]

Talbot also described the men in general as "of very respectable families." Henry King, for example, from the gentry of Georgetown, was now on his second trip with Frémont. Kern and King and Talbot, sharing the same mess, became devoted companions. Their messmate, Lieutenant Abert, was another gentleman, a product of Princeton and West Point who, recuperating from fever at Bent's Fort, passed his hours reading Horace and the New Testament in Greek.[14]

At the Lewis farm the conversations were lively; the beds, comfortable; the roof, more watertight than a wagon. Mornings after breakfast, Kern and Abert and the others rode from the farm to the camp. Along the route they passed a group of Shawnee Indian farms, neat-hewn log cabins with divided rooms comfortably furnished, fields enclosed with rail fences, draft horses and oxen, plows and wagons. These Shawnees, once the proud people of Tecumseh, now domestic and agricultural, even owners of Negro slaves, may have been the first Indians that Kern sketched, though his work in the years ahead would include dozens

13. The Jackson quotation is from E. Kern to R. Kern, June 19, 1845; the coffee quotation, from the Edward Kern Journal reprinted in James H. Simpson, *Report of Explorations across the Great Basin* (Washington, 1876), p. 482.

14. James W. Abert, "Report of Lieut. J. W. Abert, of his Examination of New Mexico, in the Years 1846–'47," in William H. Emory, *Notes of a Military Reconnoissance* (Washington, 1848), p. 419. Abert was a nature lover—his journals picture him feeding hungry dogs and protecting birds —and Dick Kern once sarcastically described him as never having grasped any idea beyond that connected with "the sweet warblers of the woods" (R. Kern to [Morton], July 3, 1850, Newberry Library). In spite of a poor academic record at West Point, he was often listed first in art, and, indeed, he later returned to the Academy as a professor of drawing. Talbot described Abert as having a particular flair for sketching and music, "amiable and agreeable but somewhat eccentric" (Talbot Letters, July 3, 1845, Library of Congress).

of Indian portraits ranging from the highly skilled Navajos and Zuñis to the Diggers of the Great Basin. As an educated Easterner, further from the reality and nearer Romantic currents, Kern was in general more sympathetic with the Indian than the frontiersmen he now joined. But such appreciation did not extend to the white missionaries among the Shawnees. "They have to put up with all the inconveniences of life such as good food, warm beds, good houses. . . . How I despise them, the Hypocrites. They civilize the Indians by mixing white Blood with the coming generation, the only way that will work. . . . If you ask an Indian if he is part white his answer is No, I'm mission, or as one told me, Methodist God damn you."[15]

During the days of preparation, Kern could practice sketching Indians even in the Frémont camp, for the expedition included a dozen Delawares whom Frémont had hired for bravery and huntsmanship. Two of them were chiefs, Swanok and Sagundai. The latter's swarthy face, flat nose and bulging lips, his hair bushing out around the ears, knife in scabbard and rifle in bend of arm, made exotic raw material. He was an intelligent man and had overcome the common primitive belief that a portrait captured and held a bit of a man's soul in bondage. And even closer at hand in Ned's own mess was Chinook, the Indian boy from the salmon waters of the Columbia River, child of the Celilo and the Deschutes, whom Frémont had carried from the Dalles to Washington and Philadelphia and now was returning to his tribe.

These first drawings during the preparatory days helped Edward sharpen new techniques. Behind him were the days of finished studio painting: the important thing now was to capture on the spot as much as he could for the record. If necessary he could write color suggestions on the drawing and wait for the finishing touches till night around the

15. E. Kern to R. Kern, June 19, 1845, Fort Sutter Papers.

fire. A few—very few—of his hundreds of sketches could be elaborated when the trip was over; but his chief goal was to act as a camera, recording the expedition as it happened. To this end these early drawings were a test.

He also took advantage of the waiting days to begin his scientific activity. While sauntering over the prairie he one day picked up some ribbed mussel shells, reminders of ancient seas; he sent them to his brother to be turned over to scientists in Philadelphia. He became most curious about the flowers, took a closer look at the new and unfamiliar ones, and probably pressed a few for future study. For a friend back home he was on the lookout for a good skin with the skull still in it, perhaps meaning a buffalo hide, most likely to be used for anatomical comparisons. So, though he complained "It is an absolute waste of time to be staying in our present place," he was already engaged in what would be the two great aspects of his life for the next fifteen years, art and science.

As Edward sketched Indians and collected shells, Alfred Waugh and John Tisdale grew apprehensive about their prospects. Several times they thought Frémont would relent and include them along with Kern, but no actual commitment was forthcoming. Waugh at length asked the Captain point blank if there were any chance they might be hired. Frémont explained the responsibility he owed the War Department, the care he must exercise in his choices, and concluded, "If you had a letter from any public character, it would be sufficient to justify my conduct in taking you." That night Waugh and Tisdale left in a hurry for St. Louis.

The two weeks in camp had ripened the men for the march. Hunters, mountaineers, guides, soldiers, and scientists had gradually assembled. In the key positions as scouts Frémont had signed not only his beloved Alexis Godey, who shared his own mess, but Lucien Maxwell, Basil Lajeunnesse, and Joseph Reddeford Walker. The horses and mules left near Westport after Frémont's last expedition stood fat, rested, and ready, and others had been bought. On the wagons the great loads took shape.

Kern had his special packing problems. Not that his belongings were excessive; on that score his friend Joseph Drayton had written good advice: "take as little with you as possible for a second shirt will sometimes be found a burthen to you." But aside from his limited supply of shirts, he had to pack large folios of thick drawing paper in boards or binders, smaller quarto and octavo pads, lead pencils and colored pencils, brushes, and tins of water colors. The major supplies of all these must go in the wagons. For daily use he organized a small waterproof India rubber knapsack in which he kept forty or fifty sheets of paper of different sizes, a few pencils and brushes, a box of colors, and a small flask of water so that coloring could be done even on the dry marches. There had been some talk that the equipment might include a daguerreotype, a likely possibility since Frémont had tried the apparatus on his first expedition. But his results had been poor, and perhaps he felt the old methods of hand sketching would suffice this time. Drayton suggested that Kern take along a camera lucida, which outlined an image for tracing on a blank sheet, feeling that Kern could thereby compete with the daguerreotype. As far as we can tell, however, neither device was taken, and some years passed before Edward Kern became proficient in photography.[16]

In the late afternoon on June 22 the animals were driven into the corral and the men assigned saddle horses and pack

16. Charles Preuss, *Exploring with Frémont: The Private Diaries of Charles Preuss,* trans. and ed. Erwin G. and Elisabeth K. Gudde (Norman, Okla., 1958), pp. 32, 35; see also Frémont's payment of bill for daguerreotype apparatus and plates, May 6, 1842, with his certification: "I certify that the above mentioned articles were received by me and used on the Surveys of the Platte and Kansas Rivers. J. C. Frémont." "Selected Records Relating to Frémont, 1842–90, from the General Accounting Office," National Archives Microfilm Publication T135, Roll 1. Joseph Drayton to Edward Kern, March 22, 1845, Huntington Library.

mules. That night Kern slept for the last time in his bed
under Lewis' roof. The following morning Frémont issued orders for marching, and "the Great North-western-
American-mule-and-pack-saddle-Exploring-Expedition" began "to catch up and saddle." The lassoing and coaxing,
the hustling and cursing, the final strapping and cinching
took the whole morning—a typical delay, long enough to
allow Ned to capture its frustrations in a drawing which
Frémont would later use in his *Memoirs*.[17] *(Fig. 6)* Not till
the early afternoon did the long caravan serpentine away.

First in line, pulled by two docile mules, bounced a
Yankee spring wagon with a square black top and buttoned,
rubber curtains. Within it lay the sextants, telescopes, thermometers, barometers, chronometers—all the scientific
apparatus of the expedition—and it went before the party
like the Ark before the children of Israel. Isaac Cooper, one
of the few who wrote accounts of the leave-taking, called
the wagon, "the Focus,—the Magnet,—the sun by day, and
the moon by night to our caravan, and ever the foremost
on the march, it was continually the object of our most
watchful and jealous care, as the repository of the wonder-
ful mechanism by means of which the world was to be en-
lightened for ages to come."

We gazed upon the little concern with a superstitious
reverence, and had an opportunity been offered us by
the Fates, to have evinced our love for botany, and the
sciences in general, by casting ourselves before this miniature car of Juggernaut in a Pawnee fight or a Root-
digger massacre, many an humble hero's name would
have adorned the niche now occupied by Arcturus . . .[18]

17. Not many of the illustrations in Frémont's *Memoirs* can be clearly
attributed, but judging from the text on pp. 483 and 484, "Moving Camp"
(p. 88) and "Tlamath Lake" (p. 441) are from Kern originals. *(Fig. 6)*
18. Montaignes, "The Plains," *9*, 222. The passages on the instrument
wagon do not appear in the manuscript version at Scripps College.

In spite of the care lavished on the wagon, before its arrival at Bent's Fort all the barometers but one were shattered.

Behind the "mystic carriage," came four heavier wagons with red and white covers drawn some by four and some by six mules. These carried the provisions and supplies. Last came the animals—the spare horses and mules and the beef cattle—surrounded by their drivers. Kern and the others rode beside and ahead of the caravan, helping where needed when wagons caught in ruts or careened down cliffs. Kern occasionally rode off to examine a curious ledge, catch a particular view, or sketch a peak from a better angle.

The expedition had marched for eight days and had camped the afternoon of July 1 when Kern saw three riders approach from the east, first on the top of a distant rise then down into a draw and up on a closer crest. He recognized Alfred Waugh and John Tisdale, and his host of many nights, farmer Lewis, acting as guide. Kern had not noticed the change in the appearance of the expedition until the newcomers provided a comparison. Beside Waugh and Tisdale, Ned and his companions, though only eight days on the trail, were unshaved, dust-caked, with "fine brandy brown" noses. Waugh had difficulty identifying former messmates.

With some interest, Kern watched Waugh ride to Frémont's tent and enter with letters in his hand. A short time later he emerged.

"We must go back."

Tisdale said nothing, but drew from his belt a small hatchet and, like a petulant child, threw it to the ground, commenting "I have no further use for that." He mounted his horse and galloped off. Waugh said a few feeble farewells, thanked Ned for his earlier help and, with Lewis, followed. They joined what Talbot had earlier called "all those sad faces—the hundreds who were more bent on going than I was and yet were doomed to disappointment."

Why Frémont turned down Waugh and Tisdale, we do not know. Of course, he had rejected many an earlier applicant, and he probably hoped that the request for credentials would discourage these later two, but if so, he underestimated the attraction his expedition exercised on such men. Then, too, he had had time to see Kern in action, to see that his drawings were accurate, that he was reliable, and that his personality fitted with the company. Frémont, in short, like so many others, had undoubtedly grown to like Ned and feel confident that he could well handle the job alone.

Waugh and Tisdale disappeared, emerged smaller on another hill, up and on. The horses left wakes in the tall grasses. Eight days on the prairie and the supplicants for positions had still followed them! But no longer. The last tie to the long stage of preparations was broken. Edward Kern could turn his sketch pad west, himself solely responsible for illustrating the Frémont expedition.

He had written his brother Dick that he was glad to be away from "civilization and brandy," a thoroughly Romantic thought, worthy of a Childe Harold or a legendary Boone. Now, except for a few picked companions, he was magnificently alone with a fascinating job to do.

Along the route to the Rockies, Frémont wrote, "we met the usual prairie incidents of Indians and large game, which furnished always wholesome excitement . . . and made a good school for the men."[19] For Kern the five weeks to Bent's Fort in present Colorado provided an especially important education. He continued drawing Indians; he sketched his first views of the buffalo, and these were exciting; but, far more significant, Frémont, Abert, and the others were teaching him the science of topography. Slowly were revealed the contents of the "mystic carriage," and the

19. Frémont, *Memoirs*, p. 425.

care with which chronometers and thermometers and barometers must be used. His predecessor, Charles Preuss, following Frémont's lead, had on the earlier expedition clucked over the instruments like a worried hen. And rightly so, for whatever scientific achievement might result would depend upon these tools. Even the collections and drawings of unknown fauna or flora would mean little without accurate concommitant knowledge of position and distance. Frémont's instruments normally included a refracting telescope, a reflecting circle, two sextants, several chronometers, two barometers (one the siphon type, the other the cistern), six thermometers, and a number of compasses. On the third expedition, although he started with more, all but one of the barometers, as we have seen, were broken before Bent's Fort. His instruments were usually chosen from among the wares of the best European and American makers and were supplemented by the elaborate mathematical tables in the *Ephemerides of the Heavens*.

Kern must have brought some mathematical knowledge with him; it is hard otherwise to understand his rapid progress with the tools of topography. At Bent's Fort, Abert and Peck, the West Point-trained engineers who could have provided constant, expert assistance for Frémont, were dispatched by him southward on a reconnaissance of the Arkansas, Canadian, and Purgatory rivers, thence to return East. In their place on the main expedition Frémont appointed Edward his assistant in charge of topography.

To be at all valuable in such a position he had to correct chronometers by astronomical observations for time, manage a telescope and the printed tables of an *Ephemerides* to determine latitude, and read the sextant, adding its triangulations to those of stars and tables to calculate the longitude, the most difficult problem of all. He had to know the various kinds of barometers and thermometers and their uses in altitudes and mean temperatures. And, more simply, there were always the odometers to note on the axles of the wagons.

A few days after Bent's Fort the first major calculations
were made where the Fontaine qui Bouit (now Fountain
Creek) flows into the Arkansas at modern Pueblo. Setting
up the portable transit, they determined longitude by moon
culminations and latitude by sextant sightings of the North
and other stars. As Frémont wrote later, ". . . it requires an
exertion of courage to take astronomical observations, and
then calculate them at night, in a linen tent, tired and cold,
and make up the notes of the day."[20] The results of this
night showed latitude 38° 15′ 18″, longitude 104° 42′ 41″,
a figure which, in terms of modern knowledge, is accurate
to the minute in latitude and to within seven minutes of
longitude, an understandable differential given the chronometers available.

But their instruments could not choose for them the best
passes through the Rockies. Their complement of scouts
had been increased at Bent's Fort by two of Frémont's
noblest, the faithful Kit Carson and the eagle-sighted Dick
Owens. But for the special problem of how best to attack
the Rockies, Frémont felt the need of even more help. At
the little settlement of Hardscrabble, tucked under the
skirts of the great mountains, he hired another guide, Old
Bill Williams. Ned was apparently intrigued with the party's new member and expatiated in his journal regarding
Williams' yellow hair, his shrunken, greasy pants, his face
streaked with vermilion like an Indian, his squaw, and his
earlier escapades at stealing horses.[21] For the expedition

20. Frémont letter, Nov. 17, 1849, in *Missouri Republican*, March 7, 1849,
folder 9, Morgan Collection. Cf. John Bigelow, *Memoir of the Life and
Public Services of John Charles Frémont* (New York, 1856), p. 360: "It
needs strong incitements to undergo the hardships and self-denial of this
kind of life . . ."

21. William Drummond Stewart, *Edward Warren* (2 vols. London, 1854),
I, 159, differs with Kern on the color of Williams' hair, but the description
of his hide pants, "lustrous with the fat of many seasons," is suspiciously
similar. George F. Ruxton, *Life in the Far West*, ed. LeRoy Hafen (Norman,
Okla., 1951), p. 113, described Old Bill, humped over his mule, in much
the way Kern did. See also Alpheus Favour, *Old Bill Williams: Mountain
Man* (Chapel Hill, N. Car., 1936), pp. 79–80.

Bill Williams performed his job well. When he left them on the other side of the mountains, Ned Kern probably thought, quite incorrectly, that he would never again see this colorful renegade from civilization.

Beyond the Great Salt Lake Frémont divided the party in order to encompass a larger reconnaissance and still reach the Sierras before snowtime. On his most recent map he had scrawled across the basin they were about to enter, "almost unknown, but believed to be filled with rivers and lakes which have no communication with the sea, deserts and oases which have never been explored, and savage tribes, which no traveler has seen or described." Across the land of this poetic concept the captain with a small group was to circle more widely, while the main party under the command of Theodore Talbot and guided by Joseph Walker would follow the Humboldt River to its sink and thence to a rendezvous at Walker's Lake. Kern, on the Humboldt route, was placed in full charge of the topography. Frémont later said that Kern commanded the party, which was not true, but the assertion betrayed Frémont's paramount interest in the topographical work as well as his estimate of Kern. From Bent's Fort, in anticipation of his increased responsibility, Edward had begun to keep a journal, a practice he would maintain throughout much of his life in the West. Daily he recorded the nature of the soil, land configurations, plant life, and occasional editorial comments, such as on the virgin character of the country.

His Indian interest, which had begun while sketching around Westport, flowered into a broader concern as he became exposed to the incredibly squalid lives of the Great Basin Diggers. He went out with Henry King, who had been with Frémont before and so knew what to expect, visiting the Indian camps near Walker's Lake. They found a dirty, primitive, fearsome people, content with a wretched diet, but Edward noted they were also clever in their construction of decoy ducks. A few days later he described a game which the Indians played with hoops and balls on sand rolled as smooth as a billiard table.[22]

The party split again after Walker's Lake, Talbot in command, Walker guiding, Kern responsible for the topography.[23] If Frémont had any doubts about Kern, he could this second time have stayed with the main party and supervised the surveying himself. Clearly he had confidence in Edward's ability. Kern had learned quickly and well from a good teacher in the field.

Each night by the incandescence of burning sage, Ned drew a field map of the day's route, the natural features, the distances, and latitudes and longitudes when determined. This was the tangible satisfaction of a man's curiosity. Within the soft leather covers of these field books an unknown or little-known land was being captured. Not only could he feel that he stood with the first white men on Pilot Peak, but also he carried away an image of that peak in his hip pocket. Night after night, page after page, the diagram expanded, a line moving inexorably west, like the course of his life, over the Rockies across the Humboldt sink through Sierra passes. Where the line would take him in California not even a man of curiosity could guess.

22. For another description of the game *(takersia)*, see Charles Rudkin, ed., *The First French Expedition to California* (Los Angeles, 1959), p. 74.

23. Frémont in his *Memoirs* (pp. 434, 439) and in his *Geographical Memoir* (1848 ed., p. 30) states or implies that Kern was in charge of the party both times; but this is not substantiated by Kern's own journal (Simpson, *Report of Explorations*, p. 477), by Kit Carson in Blanche C. Grant, ed., *Kit Carson's Own Story* (Taos, 1926), p. 67, or by Theodore Talbot's letters, all of which point to Talbot in charge, Walker as guide, and Kern directing the topography.

NOTE

The general authorities for this chapter and sources for quotations, when
not otherwise credited, are Edward Kern to Richard Kern, June 19, 1845,
Fort Sutter Papers; Alfred S. Waugh, *Travels in Search of the Elephant,*
ed. John F. McDermott (St. Louis, 1951), pp. 4–28; and Isaac Cooper (Fran-
cois des Montaignes, pseud.), "The Plains," *Western Journal and Civilian,*
9–15, o.s., 1852–56. The manuscript of this latter account is in possession
of Scripps College Library, Claremont, California. The original, which
varies from the printed version, has been used whenever possible, especially
pp. 16, 19, 27–29. John Charles Frémont, *Memoirs of My Life* (Chicago,
1886), pp. 424–26, is disappointingly brief concerning the first days of the
third expedition.

1. Richard Hovendon Kern. Daguerreotype. Huntington Library.

2. Richard H. Kern. Photograph. Smithsonian Institution.

3. Edward Kern, *Richard Kern.* Oil, 10½″ × 8½″. Smithsonian Institution.

4. Benjamin Jordan Kern. Daguerreotype. Huntington Library.

5. Edward Kern, untitled water color, April 29, 1842. Album of Mary Kern, collection of Mrs. J. M. Wolfe, Merion, Pennsylvania.

6. Edward Kern. *Moving Camp*, 1845. Lithograph. Frémont, *Memoirs* (1886).

7. Edward Kern, *Hesperomys texana.* Lithograph. Sitgreaves, *Report* (1853).

8. Edward Kern, *Numenius occidentalis.* Lithograph. Sitgreaves, *Report* (1853).

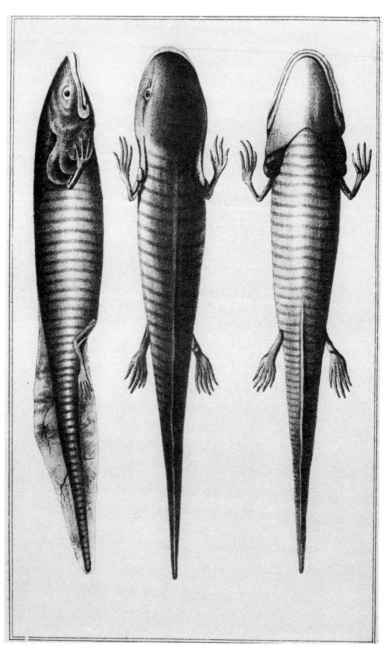

9. Richard Kern, *Fish with Legs.* Lithograph. Simpson, *Report* (1850).

10. Seth Eastman, *Female Indian of California Making Baskets, Sacramento Valley.* Water color, 8″ × 6½″, from sketch by Edward Kern. James Jerome Hill Reference Library, St. Paul.

11. Edward Kern, *Women Carrying Water and Grass Seed.* Water color, 8½″ × 6¾″.
Peabody Museum, Harvard University.

12. Seth Eastman, *Transporting Water and Grass Seed, Valley of San Joaquin, California.*
Water color, 8½″ × 6¾″, from sketch by Edward Kern. James Jerome Hill
Reference Library, St. Paul.

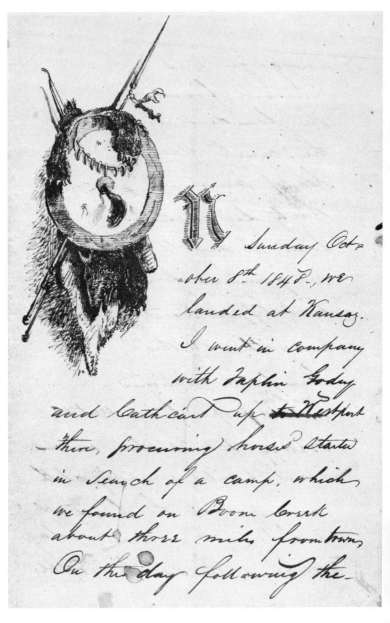

On Sunday October 8th 1848, we landed at Kansas. I went in Company with Taplin Godey and Cathcart up to Westport there, procuring horses started in search of a camp, which we found on Boon Creek about three miles from town, On the day following the

13. Edward Kern, page from Diary, 1848. Huntington Library.

Edward or Richard Kern (?), *San Luis Valley, near Sand-Hill Pass,* 1848. In publisher's prospectus for Frémont, *Memoirs.* Huntington Library.

From sketch of Richard Kern, *View of Santa Fe and Vicinity from the East,* ca. 1849. Lithograph. Simpson, *Report* (1850).

16. Edward or Richard Kern (?), *Natural Obelisks*, 1848–49. In publisher's prospectus f
Frémont, *Memoirs.* Huntington Library.

Mary

You will think it strange I have no doubt when you learn of our remaining here instead of going on with Fremont, but our tale is soon told that will give you an idea of the why and wherefore. In the first place he has broken faith with all of us. Dick and I were to have accompanied him as his artists and Dr. as Medico and Naturalist. When out we found our situation suddenly changed from what we had started for to that of Muleteros each with his number of packs and whatever work in his particular branch might turn up besides this you must believe was somewhat cutting to our dignity. Not that any of us were unwilling to assist in any work if necessity required it, but this was not the case. You know too that flattery is certainly not apart of any Kern. [illegible]

7. Edward Kern to Mary Wolfe, late February or early March, 1849. Pen and ink with water color. Huntington Library.

18. Edward or Richard Kern (?), *Copper Mines, New Mexico*, ca. 1849. Pencil sketch, 6⅞″ × 9¾′
Peabody Museum, Harvard University.

19. Richard Kern, *Indian Head* (perhaps Hosta). Diary, 1849, 2″ ×
2″. Huntington Library.

CHAPTER 2

Fort Sutter

For seven months they had tramped, mapped, and collected. Bent's Fort, the Rockies, Salt Lake, the ridges of the Great Basin, the Sierras. Hunger: horse meat and buffalo tongue. Thirst: sweet streams one day, alkali or salt water another. Christmas on the wild eastern slopes of the Sierra with a Yule log of yucca and dinner of a tired mule. A New Year's feast on acorns, a "swinish food" to Ned. Indian attacks, mosquitoes, fleas, a greasy beard, and emerging ribs. But withal, a growing pile of charts and sketches: *Erodium cicutarium, Fremontia vermicularis, Platanus occidentalis,* and water colors which caught mountains grown with pines and aspen dimmed by mists. Pilot Peak: latitude 41° 00′ 28″; longitude 114° 11′ 09″; mean temperature 40° at sunrise. And the Jersey wagon, its barometers and sextants, going on before.

The work and the ache were one thing; the way the Frenchmen, swinging along an early-morning trail, would break into an old patois song was another. And Ned's personality, like the songs, was a boost. The greatest of the Santa Fe traders, William Becknell, once described what it meant to have a man like Ned in company: "the hiliarity [sic] and sociability of this gentleman often contributed to disperse the gloomy images which very naturally presented themselves on a journey of such uncertainty and adventure."[1] And there were plenty of occasions for tomfoolery—mess number eight stealing the brandy from mess number seven, which had won it in a shooting match; practical jokes, and banter. These were things Ned loved.

After the rendezvous and second division, Old Joe Walker guided the Talbot–Kern section down the defile east of the Sierra toward the pass which he had pioneered a dozen years before. Here, in what came to be called Walker's Pass, Edward took a frightened look southward across the Mojave, "a continued plain of sand, relieved only by an occasional hill of burnt rock" and "Jeremiah trees,"[2] and the men turned down a clear, unnamed river into the Valley of California. "It lay beneath us, bright in the sunshine, gay and green" through warm January days which had already brought out the young grass and a few early lupine.[3]

Frémont with fifteen men had meanwhile in December crossed the Sierra directly, fortunate in a mild winter, and dropped into John Sutter's fort on the Sacramento. The two sections had planned to meet in the San Joaquin Valley on a river called the Lake Fork which they would recognize because it emptied into Tulare Lake. Frémont came south to the stream now called King's and found a herd of three hundred elk grazing the new grass along the river but no trace of his men. By the middle of January he returned north where he assumed that, if they were safe, Talbot, Kern, and the others would eventually seek him out.

1. As quoted in R. L. Duffus, *Santa Fe Trail* (London, 1930), p. 78.
2. Later to be named Joshua Trees.
3. Edward Kern Journal in Simpson, *Report of Explorations*, pp. 484, 485.

The missing group had meanwhile waited on the river down which they had marched from the mountains and which also ultimately flowed into Tulare Lake, hence the confusion. Frémont later named the new stream the Kern in honor of Edward, and so the mistaken camp in January 1846 resulted in Edward Kern's most enduring commemoration. Subsequently the river's name was applied to a lake and a city and a county. But Edward himself saw his namesake, the river, for no more than three weeks. After that time the party moved north to find its captain, who was eventually located with the help of a hulking mountaineer, Le Gros Fallon, at San Jose near the foot of the Bay.

Frémont had received tacit permission from the California–Mexican authorities for his scientific pursuits on their soil. "Among civilized nations," said one man at the time, "scientific expeditions are always treated with courtesy and hospitality, even if they are in a country actually at war with their own."[4] But later in that tense year of 1846, when Frémont seemed to be overstaying his welcome and camping unduly near the capital at Monterey, General Castro summarily ordered the party to leave. Frémont, feigning outrage, dramatically raised the United States flag over a hastily built fort in the Gavilan Mountains. Neither side judged the time right for shooting, however, and a few days later, the Ides of March, the expedition was retiring northward "slowly and growlingly."

Near the rocky banks of Klamath Lake early in May, Archibald Gillespie, a lieutenant of Marines, overtook Frémont with messages from Washington: the captain, according to his own account, was to test the California people, "to conciliate their feelings in favor of the United States, and to find out, with a view to counteracting, the designs of the British Government upon that country." In the dark forests of the Klamath, Frémont and his men thus became "a pawn,

4. Joseph Revere, *A Tour of Duty in California* (New York, 1849), p. 46.

and like a pawn . . . pushed forward to the front at the opening of the game."[5] War between the United States and Mexico was not yet declared when Gillespie left Washington,
but the air smelled strongly of it. Frémont, knowing he had
the active support of several senators, the Secretary of the
Navy, and Manifest Destiny, was hardly averse to being
pushed to the front, to grasping for his country what he
feared might otherwise run like a frightened deer toward
England. "I saw the way opening clear before me. War
with Mexico was inevitable; and a grand opportunity now
presented itself to realize in their fullest extent the far-
sighted views of Senator Benton, and make the Pacific
Ocean the western boundary of the United States."[6] The
exploring expedition which entered the Oregon woods with
barometer and sextant emerged an agent of conquest, and
Edward Kern returned to the Sacramento a soldier.

Like a multi-forked stream converging on a narrow canyon, at least three sources contributed to the crisis in
California. First, the mere trickle of control which mean-
dered toward the province from Mexico City had left a
power vacuum. Secondly, the local administration in California had for decades been rife with conflict. In 1846
General Castro in Monterey and Governor Pico in Los
Angeles each rallied forces to dispute the claims of the
other. Concurrently, within the province a movement was
already under way to loose the tie with Mexico and estab-
lish an independent republic. Thirdly, there were conflict-
ing foreign claims resulting from the residence of aliens,
and widespread fears of foreign annexation—perhaps
France, perhaps Prussia, perhaps England, perhaps the

5. For one statement of the content of the message, see J. C. Frémont,
"California Claims," 30th Cong., 1st Sess., Sen. Rep. Com. no. 75 (Washing-
ton, 1848), p. 12. See also John A. Hussey, "The Origin of the Gillespie
Mission," *Calif. Hist. Soc. Quarterly, 19* (1940), 43–58, and Allan Nevins,
Frémont (New York, 1939), pp. 238–48. The quotations are from Frémont,
Memoirs, pp. 489, 536.
6. Frémont, *Memoirs,* p. 490.

United States. If any California faction had approached England for protection in 1846, the British ministry, embarking now on its historic adventure in free trade, would undoubtedly have repudiated the idea. But Californians did not know that. Her Majesty's warships rode anchor at strategic points along the coast, and Frémont thought their presence spoke only too eloquently.

The nearly eight hundred settlers of the Sacramento Valley among whom Frémont now marched agreed with him that if any protecting was to be done, the United States should do it. They feared rumors that the provincial regime, even in its weakness, might try to evict American aliens. And worse, the same treacherous Mexicans might incite the local Indian tribes to burn houses, destroy wheat fields, and rape American women. During these months, whenever an Indian farm worker disappeared by night, his farmer-employer imagined a wild mountain rendezvous and savage rites in preparation for attack.

Moving down the Sacramento, Frémont's band, technically a part of the United States Army, thus was eagerly watched by both American and Mexican. Frémont knew that if he were forced to march south on declaration of war, the American settlers on the Sacramento would be unprotected. His first move, therefore, was a premeditated attack on Indian rancherias, burning huts and food, killing and scattering the inhabitants. The attacks probably bothered Edward but little. He was rapidly becoming disenchanted with Indians. He had now known months on the trail under the sneak attacks and petty thieveries of the Diggers of the Great Basin, and considered these California Indians perpetrators of the same kind of theft and treachery.

With the Indians momentarily quieted, Frémont, interpreting his instructions in the broadest way, slowly and adroitly maneuvered the forces of independence to an eruption in the Bear Flag Revolt. Some thirty-odd men, led by the rawboned Ezekial Merritt, the pontifical William B.

Ide, and the towering Kentuckian Robert Semple, moved
on Sonoma in the daybreak of June 14. They took prisoner
the leaders of the town—General Mariano G. Vallejo, his
brother, and Colonel Victor Prudon—raised a flag on which
they painted a comically crude bear, and proclaimed a republic. The next day they marched their prisoners, with
Jacob P. Leese, Mariano Vallejo's brother-in-law, as interpreter, overland to Frémont's camp on the American River.
Frémont thought it wise to incarcerate the prisoners, including Leese, nearby at Fort Sutter, and he so directed,
proceeding to the fort to talk with Sutter himself about
the matter.

John Sutter and Frémont were old acquaintances. In
1844 at the Sutter board Frémont had revived the tired,
bedraggled spirits of his second expedition. He could still
remember the Indian maidens serving feasts of roast veni-
son, salad, and Rhine wine, and already this year he had
formed fresher memories of the host of the Sacramento.
But Sutter was a Mexican citizen, legally if not by whole-
hearted sentiment. He had proclaimed himself a neutral
and he resented Frémont's present disturbance in the valley.
Sutter wanted peace and good business in his empire; Frémont portended neither. Sutter now protested the bringing
of the prisoners as a violation of his neutrality. Frémont
spoke firmly to his bewhiskered friend and convinced him
to allow an Army commander on his property to supervise
the Sonoma prisoners. Frémont wished to preserve his own
freedom of action and avoid the open commitment which
his personal command in the fort might imply: he maintained his camp near the river, and placed Edward Kern in
charge of the prisoners at Fort Sutter.

Kern was a more logical choice than he might seem. His
topographical work, particularly the two special assignments, had proved his reliability. His friendliness and humor would smooth the rough going in relations with Sutter.
And from the standpoint of probable fighting around Mon-

terey or to the south, an artist—and especially an artist with epilepsy—was, to say the least, dispensable.

Finally, on July 4, with still no word of war with Mexico, Frémont openly took charge of the revolt by organizing the California Battalion at Sonoma. In this heterogeneous collection of explorers, Bear Flaggers, and discontented rabble, later officially recognized by Commodore Robert Stockton as a fighting arm of the United States, Edward Kern was signed as a first lieutenant on detached duty.

On July 12, a few days after the declaration of war became known in California, Kern's orders were expanded to give him full command of Fort Sutter. Frémont clarified the status with specific instructions to "iron and confine any person who shall disobey your orders—shoot any person who shall endanger the safety of the place."[7] Ned thus at the age of twenty-three wrote his brother Dick: "Little did I think when sitting at home in our office in F[ilbert] St. that I would ever raise to be a Mil. character, a rale Commandante of a Fort, with power to do as I pleased and shoot people if they do not obey me, and all that sort of thing."[8]

There were some aspects of his command, however, which did not delight him. The garrison which he took over from Sutter was composed of about fifty "runaway seamen and Indians," Hawaiian Kanakas, and Mexican gauchos; Kern commented sourly, "I would not march through Coventry with them!" He was little better impressed with the local citizens. Lansford Hastings, immigrant leader and eager revolutionist, he called "as big an ass as runs," and in the same letter to his brother he cartooned the Bear Flaggers as disorganized, wrangling, gawky bumpkins. But far worse than the men, Ned found in the fort—in the beds, in the

7. Frémont to E. Kern, July 12, 1846, Huntington Library. Montgomery reiterated Kern's appointment in orders to Lt. J. S. Missroon, Aug. 1, 1846, in R. F. Stockton, et al, Orders, Leidesdorff Papers, Huntington Library.
8. E. Kern to R. Kern, July 27 [?], 1846, Huntington Library.

walls, rising from the floors and corners—"the most ungodly
hord of the largest and hardest to catch–highest jumping
–and hard biting, putting-your-finger-on-and-not-to-[be]-
found fleas that have ever worried man since the days of
Adam."

On the morning of July 11, 1846, Ned watched a United
States flag rise for the first time over Fort Sutter. The rough
garrison stood in a wobbly line before the flagstaff which
extended above the peaked roof of the center building, and
the crackling of their rifles was drowned by Sutter's cannon
on the ramparts, booming salutes to the flag until nearly
all the glass in the fort was shattered. The banner's blue
field bore twenty-seven stars, not yet including one for
newly admitted Texas. A few days later Commodore Montgomery at Yerba Buena sent over a small package of muslin
from which to fashion another star: impolitic indeed would
be the forgetting of a new state which had boldly carved its
independence out of Mexican sovereignty—the present situation in California carried too many obvious parallels.

Inside the central building—flag at the front and fleas
inside—Kern set up his quarters, installing his meager belongings, the rubber knapsack of paints and pencils, blankets, rifle and pistols. In the months ahead he probably
spent as much time on the bed as at the desk in this little
office, for Ned, naturally as thin as a consumptive, was ill
during much of the late summer and early fall. A very
short time after the raising of the flag, he was down with
what was called a raging fever and ague. He was not alone;
many of the garrison, including the Bear Flag prisoners,
were similarly stricken. In their petition for release, Sal-
vador Vallejo (who called it "black fever"), Prudon, and
Leese made a special plea to consider their illness in "a
place as notoriously unhealthy as this." The surgeon of the
U. S. S. *Portsmouth,* then at anchor in San Francisco Bay,
sent over some Dover's powder, to be continued with any
laudanum or opium compound, and cautioned Ned to look

to his diet, avoiding corn bread and beans. But to little avail. As late as November, the local sheriff, George Mc-Kinstry, wrote, "our friend Capt. Kern is in bed by my side (in the office) shaking finely with the chills . . . ."[9] Some of these attacks may have been epileptic, though no one recorded them as such.

In his active moments, Kern's talents at drawing and topography were suddenly less important than his humor and personality, for his new problems were neither artistic nor scientific, but highly personal. He faced the animosity which any invader arouses. He had to cope with excitable farmers worried about Indian dangers, with Indians incensed over swelling numbers of settlers, with immigrants issuing by the hundreds down the mountain passes. After war became a reality, he had to recruit able men, both settlers and fresh immigrants, dispatch them to the fighting fronts, and care for their women and children. To such jobs of personal relations and organization Kern brought no training whatsoever, only a likable personality.

His most immediate problem was John Sutter, a gentleman, but one whose manners and side-whiskers could not wholly conceal his discomfort at being in a secondary position on his own property. "I can assure you," he wrote, "it is not very pleasant to have another as Comander in his own house and establishemt [sic]."[10] Sutter, who loved the colored ribbons of his Mexican officer's uniform, now found himself commanded by an explorer in skin trousers—a mere boy and, to make matters worse, one who looked down from a six-foot height onto Sutter's stocky shortness. This upstart now ordered him to keep tedious records for the

9. Petition of prisoners for release, Aug. 5, 1846; Dr. A. A. Henderson to E. Kern, July 26, 1846; Fort Sutter Papers, Huntington Library. McKinstry to P. B. Reading, Nov. 2, 1846, typed copy in Reading Collection, Calif. State Library; the typescript reads "Capt. Kerrie," but I have assumed this is a typing error for Kern or Kerne.

10. John Sutter to W. A. Leidesdorff, Aug. 14, 1846, Leidesdorff Papers, Huntington Library.

garrison and gratuitously allotted him rations and fifty dollars a month in pay. His irritation must have been deep.
Many years later in his reminiscences he labeled Edward
and his men common spies, Frémont a tyrant, and his officers a boorish lot. "I remained in absolute command," he
asserted, and pushed, it would seem, an embarrassing episode out of his thoughts forever.[11]

Yet at the time there was no trouble, no overt dispute,
no violent feuds or harsh words, and for this Ned must be
held largely responsible. The two men shared meals in
Sutter's own dining room, welcoming visitors like Frémont
or Edwin Bryant, the journalist, to the benches around the
unfinished wood table. Soup was served in china bowls and
eaten with silver spoons, and there were always platters of
roast meat, highly seasoned with onions, and plenty of
cheese and butter and melons. For this Kern could be grateful to Sutter, but for what could Sutter thank Kern? He
could only appreciate Ned's joking nature. Ned enjoyed
Sutter's irrepressible, embroidered stories of exploits as a
Mexican captain and he would try to cap each one with a
taller tale or a pun. They joked their way through the situation to such an extent that a few years later, long before he
recorded his more bitter reminiscences, Sutter wrote of his
days with Kern in 1846 ". . . how many hearty laughs we
had, and enjoyed ourselves, in our old poor times."[12]

The Sonoma prisoners were another problem in human
relations. Mariano Vallejo was undoubtedly furious. The
one man in California who, with Larkin, was most anxious
for independence was now, with relatives and friends,
thrown into prison after the first fumbling move toward
that independence. And Ned Kern was his jailer. In the

11. J. Sutter, *Sutter's Own Story*, ed. E. G. Gudde (New York, 1936), pp.
172, 175–76. The New Helvetia Diary broke off abruptly shortly after Kern
arrived. The silence may be explained by a lack of time for writing, but
it seems more likely that Sutter simply did not wish to have his humiliating
position recorded.

12. J. Sutter to R. Kern, Jan. 10, 1852, Huntington Library.

fort Vallejo's body raged with fever, and his spirits must
have been no less feverish. Yet when he was finally released
in August, he had nothing but kind words for Kern's treatment and good company. The two must have talked about
all manner of things, including literature and science, for
in gratitude Vallejo sent Edward gifts according to their
discussions: a copy of *Don Quixote*, "my small thermome-
ter, a curious lamp-burner, and some cigars, so that you
will remember a prisoner friend."[13]

For a while in June and July the fort was a gay place.
Though Henry King and Theodore Talbot and the other
friends of the expedition were soon on the march, Ned was
making new acquaintances. A man called Charles Pickett
came in shortly after Ned took command, and although he
stayed no more than two weeks before returning to Yerba
Buena, he later came often to the Sacramento, and the two
became friends. Pickett was a young, gray-eyed wanderer
with a winning Virginia manner, a caustic wit, and a per-
petual fund of fresh anecdotes. Like Ned a bachelor all his
life, he considered himself an authority on women and
would pass judgment on a new town: "No pretty girls here
though plenty of accommodating ones."[14]

Enough women lived around the fort to provide Ned and
Charles Pickett with chances to compare notes. There was
Sarah Montgomery, called a "black bottle" woman, who
had been brought by her gunsmith husband to live in the
fort for the duration of the crisis. Ned seemed fond of her
—at least she was referred to as his "particular friend." The
fondness apparently persisted, for late that year he was still
doodling her name all over the payrolls, drawing her round
form, writing "Jesus Christ Sarah Montgomery" and, care-
less of her married state, even practicing "Sarah Kern." It

13. M. Vallejo to E. Kern, Aug. 14, 1846, Huntington Library; trans.
Haydée Noya.
14. As quoted in Lawrence Clark Powell, *Philosopher Pickett* (Berkeley,
1942), p. 136.

may have been Sarah whom Pickett referred to in a later note to Ned: "I suspect from the tone of your letter (and am sorry for you) that some fair one has been unkind, and not presented front to meet your bayonet charge. Don't despair old fellow, but at 'em again! 'better luck next time' —'no use in crying.' "[15]

Kern's chief concern, however, was always his obligation to the fort, and he must have deduced from Sutter's stories that the adobe walls would not long remain quiet of hostile Indian shouts. Sutter, as long-time magistrate of the district, was technically responsible for the Indians, but the present danger of Indian uprisings distracting the war effort was Kern's worry as well. On the eighth of September an exhausted courier rode from the north with breathless reports of one thousand Walla Walla Indians entering the Sacramento Valley bent on war. Their chief's son, Elijah (christened by Methodist missionaries), on an earlier visit to California had been killed in a brawl and buried in the fields by the American River. The father, Piopiomoxmox, called by the whites Yellow Serpent, had armed with rifles a revenge party of nearly two hundred and led them with their families down the long trail from the Columbia to the Sacramento. The rumors left the valley's farmers terrified.

Kern acted quickly. He dispatched riders to Commander Montgomery at Yerba Buena, and Montgomery, in charge of all northern forces, ordered aid to converge on Fort Sutter from Sonoma, San Jose, and Monterey.[16] Commodore Stockton, Pacific commander, himself hurried to Yerba Buena, and Montgomery sent Lieutenant Missroon to Sonoma to direct a relief expedition from that post. Kern, however, had expressed direct word to the commander at Sonoma, Joseph Revere, a young Navy lieutenant from the

15. Powell, p. 149.
16. For full details of the network of official actions, see John A. Hussey and George W. Ames, "California Preparations to Meet the Walla Walla Invasion, 1846," *Calif. Hist. Soc. Quarterly, 21* (1942), pp. 9–21.

Portsmouth. Revere set off with his garrison for Fort Sutter immediately. This grandson of Paul Revere, already an
eighteen-year veteran of sea battles with pirates and slavers,
had found tedious indeed his temporary assignment commanding a tiny, flea-bitten garrison. Furthermore, he hated
the Indians, likened them to spiders, and was delighted at
the chance to crush them.

Meanwhile at Fort Sutter, Kern sent Indian spies northward and couriers in all directions to recruit the settlers
for defense of the valley. He and Sutter now enrolled the
farmers by the dozens. When Revere rode in with his men
the following day, the fort buzzed with preparation: the
drilling of amicable Indians, the shouting of muleteers,
shoeing of horses, rifle practice. Beside the gateway hung an
Indian scalp with streaming black hair, a talismanic incen-
tive to activity, for the particular Indian from whom it had
been carved was rumored to have been sent by Castro to
fire the wheat fields and murder Sutter. Within twenty-four
hours of Revere's arrival, one hundred fifty white and nearly three hundred friendly Indian fighting men were camped
outside the fort on the banks of the American River.

Revere could hardly wait for the fight to begin. Together
he and Kern probably buoyed one another's enthusiasm,
adding "zest to the sport in prospect." Then, on the morning the force was to move, just before the order to mount,
Yellow Serpent himself with a small band of his chief warriors, peaceful and unarmed, appeared through the oaks on
the opposite bank of the river. The Americans stood like
disconsolate boys looking on the last successful efforts of the
firemen. The Indians rode quietly to the fort and explained
that they had come to talk. Kern and Revere could do
nothing but assent: a circle formed, and Yellow Serpent
began.

"I have come from the forests of Oregon with no hostile
intentions. You can see that I speak the truth, because I
have brought with me only forty warriors, with their women

and little children, and because I am here with few followers
and without arms."[17] His speech which followed was long,
but it concealed an even longer story. Yellow Serpent had
actually marched from the Columbia with an armed force
of two hundred men bent on revenge and destruction. It is
probably true that Kern's forthright defensive action discouraged the enraged father and caused him to reconsider
his hostile intent. Facing certain defeat, he swallowed pride,
assumed a pacific mien, and assuaged his sorrow for Elijah
with no more than a graveside visit.

Edward, loath perhaps to disappoint Revere in his desire
for sport and conscious of his own obligations to protect
the Sacramento settlers, used his recruits for a demonstration to all the Indians in the valley and marched up the
river past Indian rancherias as far as the Buttes. It gave
Ned a chance to see again the native habitats, and he took
the opportunity to sketch the primitive huts and the squaws
gathering seeds. *(Figs. 10–12)*

Meanwhile during September 1846, the conquest, which
had been going so successfully for the Americans, was
suddenly wrenched by an insurrection to the south throwing Los Angeles back into the hands of the Mexicans. The
Americans retreated ignominiously. Men in the north were
needed quickly for a march southward under Frémont.
Commander Montgomery relayed to Kern the first official
news of the southern revolt: Kern must vigilantly secure
the fort and, because of his crucial position relative to the
Sacramento Valley and the passes used by most immigrants,
he must make special efforts at recruitment. As Revere
said, echoing his grandfather, "Call in *all* Americans to
Arms . . . Enroll *all* for the common defence for the enemy
threaten the utter extermination of *all* Americans."[18]

As early as August, Kern had called for volunteers and
searched for mounts. Now he drafted Le Gros Fallon, the

17. Revere, *Tour of Duty,* p. 157.
18. J. Revere to E. Kern, Oct. 17, 1846, Fort Sutter Papers.

strapping Irish trapper who had helped the Talbot–Kern
party find Frémont earlier that year and who now happened
to be at Fort Sutter, to ride north and round up men on the
upper Sacramento. Within two days Fallon had mustered
twenty-two and expected to find more. They straggled into
the fort singly and in little groups, and Edward enlisted
them, supplied them as best he could, and sent them on to
Montgomery or Frémont.

On the morning of October 29 Kern received an offer of
additional help inscribed on two sides of a small sheet of
paper:

> We the undersigned offer to the commandant of
> Fort Sacramento the following propositions for raising
> volunteers.
>
> 1st   We will seperate and ride in different direc-
> tions where emigrants are located and engage them as
> volunteers . . . .
>
> 2nd   We are authorized to take all horses needed
> for said companies . . . giving receipt for same.
>
> 3rd   Such emigrants as have families, and will vol-
> unteer, their families are to be furnished with flour
> and meats by the government, to be deducted from the
> pay of such volunteers. The families if they desire it
> are to be quartered in Fort Sacramento, during the
> period of enlistment.
>
> 4th   We are to be authorized to raise as many In-
> dians as we may deem safe to accompany us. . . .
>
> 5th   The white volunteers to receive the same pay
> as those heretofore enlisted, viz Twenty five dollars per
> month, with horse, saddle and bridle.
>
> 6th   Those who have ammunition, saddle and bri-
> dle will use the same at expense of government.[19]

19. E. Bryant, et al., to E. Kern, Oct. 28, 1846, Fort Sutter Papers.

It was signed by five men, who had sat in the fort during the rainy night of October 28 drafting the proposal. They were all immigrants of that summer, all genuinely worried over the prospects in California. Edwin Bryant, a vigorous Kentucky journalist, probably dominated the group. Richard Jacob, a friend of Bryant from Louisville, would one day win the hand of a daughter of Thomas Hart Benton; Benjamin Lippincott, a gambler by vocation, would serve in the California constitutional convention; Andrew Grayson, a Louisianan, had already settled with his wife and child on the upper Sacramento; James Reed, a wealthy Scotch–Irish merchant with a haughty Polish strain, had left Illinois with the Donner party that summer, had killed a man on the trail, and had been expelled from the Donner company as a result.

Edward approved the proposal immediately. Bryant and the others, with the exception of Reed, began scouring the country, and a new supply of volunteers and families began dribbling into the fort.

Fort Sutter had become a funnel of recruitment. Kern stood at the neck encouraging the volume and directing the flow toward the military needs. Revere did the same kind of job at Sonoma. But Fort Sutter was more strategically placed than Sonoma because it could not only draft settlers but snare immigrants. The overlanders—some five hundred stumbled through the Sierras into the Sacramento Valley that summer—were surprisingly receptive to enlistment. After months of unsettling trek, they may have found the twenty-five dollars a month irresistible; they may have been swayed, too, by the information that prospects of land concessions were dimming under the Mexican regime and that their service might help secure their projected homes under a stable government.

Frémont marched south toward the end of November with 428 men. Fort Sutter and Sonoma had supplied over ninety and Bryant's plan had netted seventy or eighty more.

Adding the Indians, one might reasonably say that Fort Sutter supplied over thirty per cent of the force which marched south.[20] Commander Montgomery, understandably, wrote Kern particular compliments on his recruiting success. He might well have commented also on Ned's success in keeping fifty to sixty white women and children and one hundred Indians fed and clothed while their men were marching.

Edward continued recruitment till the middle of January, when he received word that Los Angeles had been retaken, the Mexicans having surrendered to his captain at Cahuenga. About the same time, on the eighteenth or nineteenth of January, he received news of chilling contrast. A segment of an immigrant party had staggered into Johnson's Ranch, the first settlement past the mountains, with little life left; eight frozen bodies littered the trail behind. Only by eating human flesh had five women and two men rallied the strength to force through. Beyond the summit of the pass they had left sixty-four men, women, and children, the main body of the Donner Party, huddling in tents and hastily built cabins, near starvation.

Ned felt at least partly responsible for the relief of these people. He called to the fort armory all the men in the area and asked for volunteers to take aid, and on the last day of January, seven men under Aquilla Glover plodded on horses and mules out of the fort, crossed the swollen American River, and disappeared into the oak thickets. During February other relief activities took shape. Commander Joseph Hull (Montgomery's successor) in Yerba Buena received moving letters from Kern, a meeting was held in the bay city to raise funds, and in time a small body of men and material reached Johnson's Ranch.

Toward the end of February Ned himself moved out to

20. Edwin Bryant, *What I Saw*, p. 347; Montgomery to Kern, Nov. 8, 1846, Fort Sutter Papers. For the care of families at the Fort, see E. Kern to A. Gillespie, March 11, 1853, Fort Sutter Papers.

the base of the rescue operations. Probably intending to be gone for some weeks, he left in command of the garrison George McKinstry, sheriff of the district, in whom he had found a good friend. The party of seven under Aquilla Glover had received a modicum of reinforcement at Johnson's Ranch and, fearing to waste time waiting for others, had beaten their way into the snow. They had reached the camps of the Donners, found death, mutilated bodies, and cannibalism, and had started back with twenty-one of the strongest survivors—fifteen of them children and two of them only three years old. On March 1, shortly after Edward arrived on Bear River, the vanguard of this relief party came in, starving, flayed by cold, their feet swollen and bloody. Edward set up a well-stocked way-camp about midpoint between the edge of the mountains and Johnson's Ranch. Here he did what he could for the survivors as they emerged from the foothills on the last sixty miles to Fort Sutter.[21]

The fact that Ned did not himself join any of the several parties which thereafter pushed into the mountains to help the Donners seems to indicate his lack of heart in the project. James Reed at the fort in October had painted the Donner Party as a quarrelsome, dissident group whose present plight was the direct result of bickerings and shirkings and loiterings. Sheriff McKinstry concurred and even wrote Ned rather flippantly to hurry home and "look out for those man eating women." Furthermore, Ned undoubtedly felt that his position at Fort Sutter demanded a closer touch with men and events than isolated weeks with a rescue crew would allow.

Such a feeling of responsibility for his position at the fort was justified by a letter which two Indians from the garrison brought to camp on March 5. If Ned had any intention of joining a relief party—the one, for instance, that

21. G. McKinstry to J. B. Hull, in *California Star*, March 13, 1847; Bryant, *What I Saw*, p. 232. For Kern's activities, see Fort Sutter Papers, MSS 104–14.

left Johnson's Ranch on March 7—this letter from George
McKinstry quickly changed his mind.

Fort Sacramento, March 4th, '47

Dear Kern,

Enclosed I send you copy of petition from citizens
in the upper Valley the original I have put with your
papers in your office. It was brought down by John Williams and Sam Smith and arrived here at sundown yes-
terday and as they appear to think their "sufferings is
intolerable and cries alloued for releif" I have thought
proper to send you the document by two of the soldiers
as you may think it necessary to leave your mountain
camp and return to your station on the banks of the
Sacramento. . . .

In the enclosure, sixteen settlers on Mill Creek, high in the
Sacramento valley near Lassen's, informed Kern that "the
Indians are assembling together and have commensed killing cattle . . . and driven a portion into the mountian. The
Indians are vary numerous and if we cannot get assistance
the probable consequence will be that we will be forced to
abandon our farms and leave our property to the murcy
of the Indians purhaps something worse."[22]

So the Sacramento tribes were again causing trouble for
the commandant of Fort Sutter. Edward sent to McKinstry
for as much of the garrison as could be spared, and when
they rode in he moved up the valley with his ragged soldiers.
Wherever he found settlers, by primitive cabins, in the
midst of new fields green with spring wheat, he heard the
same story—armed Indian bands raiding at night, cattle
disappearing, even murders of friendly natives who worked
for the whites. Military recruiting had drained the area of
manpower, and the mountain tribes were taking advantage

22. G. McKinstry to E. Kern, March 4, 1847; Daniel Sill, et al., to E.
Kern, Feb. 28, 1847; Fort Sutter Papers.

of that fact. They were often joined by valley Indians, normally dependent on and well-disposed toward the whites, but now drifting, unemployed, because so many ranchers were off in the Army.

Edward led his troop into the hills and early one morning surprised a small Indian mountain village. The natives offered no resistance and admitted thefts of cattle. Kern left a guard over them while he led his crew to a larger roost nearby. Here there was fighting and four Indians were killed before the others surrendered. He took a number of prisoners back to his camp in the valley, where he lectured them all on the importance of the change of government and the consequences of their disobedience to law.

It is doubtful that the effect of Ned's lecture was very considerable. He continued his foray into most of the Indian villages of the area, killing a total of ten Indians, and this more than the lecturing probably forestalled some violence. But he had no illusions about lasting reformation. On his return he suggested in a letter to Commander Hull that a temporary Army garrison be established to protect both settlers and immigrants.[23] It was the kind of solution he would later participate in himself while helping the Army shield New Mexico from Navajo and Apache.

During his raids on what he called the "naked Diggers," Edward again carried his pencils, and he returned with more sketches of California natives—buxom women, unclothed except for light grass skirts, gathering, cleaning, or carrying grass seed. Some years later in 1853, Henry Schoolcraft asked Ned about California Indian customs, and as an artist Kern responded with some appreciative comments on the crafts: "In the manufacture of their baskets and socks, they display much neatness and taste, particularly in those covered with feathers, generally, from the summer duck, and scalps of the red-headed woodpecker. . . ." But his punitive marches had left a lasting impression, for he also said, "Treachery and theft, as with all Indians, form

23. E. Kern to J. B. Hull, March 30, 1847, Fort Sutter Papers.

part of their creed."[24] What illusions about Indians he had held before 1845 were now long vanished.

In this period he continued collecting natural specimens, particularly birds, which were becoming one of his primary scientific loves. While in camp on Bear Creek waiting for the Donner survivors, he caught a falcon which he added to his collection and which remains today a type specimen for ornithologists.[25]

The California conquest was drawing to an end. In April, the California Battalion, of which Kern was technically a part, disbanded in Los Angeles. Ned had grown tired of the military life and as early as February had written Pickett, his friend of early days at the fort, that he was ready to leave "Othello's occupation." But through May he was still closing the Fort Sutter accounts with Commander Hull, a bookkeeping task which always gave him trouble and must have been distasteful to a temperament like Ned's, but a job which he dutifully finished, even retaining personal copies of the payrolls and garrison documents.

He kept duplicates because he was increasingly aware of the growing hostility toward his commander. Frémont, whose lieutenant-colonel status was less than a year old, was clearly outranked by a later arrival, Brigadier General Kearny, but Frémont denied Kearny's right to command him, taking his orders instead from Commodore Stockton, who had commissioned the California Battalion before any Army general was anywhere near California. General Kearny on his arrival had ordered the lieutenant colonel to make no changes in the California Battalion without the general's sanction; to which the lieutenant colonel answered, ". . . until you and Commodore Stockton adjust

24. Henry R. Schoolcraft, *Historical and Statistical Information, Respecting the History, Condition and Prospects of the Indian Tribes of the United States,* 5 (6 vols. Philadelphia, 1851–57), 80, 216–17, 649–50. A few of Kern's California sketches are in the Peabody Museum of Archaeology and Ethnology, Harvard University.

25. *Falco nigripes* Cassin, Academy of Natural Sciences, Philadelphia; letter from Herbert Friedman to R. Hine, Aug. 5, 1959.

between yourselves the question of rank, where I respectfully think the difficulty belongs, I shall have to report and receive orders as herefore, from the commodore."[26] From Kearny's viewpoint this was mutiny. Kern realized that Frémont in the months ahead would probably call upon him for evidence.

The Frémont–Kearny–Stockton bickering was a good indication that the real job of the conquest was over. California was won, military government established. When the California Battalion was discharged, the exploring expedition, whose departure from Westport seemed so long ago, was theoretically reconstituted. But its members had scattered, and when Frémont requested a return east with the expedition's remaining handful of men at his own expense, Kearny, who planned a court-martial for Frémont, flatly refused to let him march independently. At Kearny's command, Frémont with his expedition was to travel deferentially a few miles behind the party of the general.

Ned, along with eighteen other members of the original sixty, tagged along to the rendezvous on the Sacramento in June. Le Gros Fallon, the first man Edward had met in California, was there, now guiding the party home. At Fort Sutter Ned and Henry King, who had marched south with Frémont during the conquest, spent the waiting days riding into the canyons, watching the dogwood fleck the green hillsides. When the trek across the continent began, Kern and King got only as far as Bear River, where the Donner relief camp once stood. There amid the ghosts of starving immigrants and thieving Diggers, Edward fell too ill to continue the trip. It may have been epilepsy or it may have been a recurrence of the fever which had plagued him throughout his days in California. King was also taken ill. Perhaps neither of them wanted much to leave California anyway. They stayed for a while in Bear Valley, then turned back to Sacramento. Edward kept his Fort Sutter papers with him

26. U.S. War Dept., *Proceedings of the Court-martial in the Trial of Lieut. Colonel Frémont* (30th Cong., 1st Sess., Sen. Ex. Doc. 33), p. 6.

and, because of his illness, neither he nor the papers figured in the Frémont court-martial.

Kern passed the summer in Yerba Buena and Monterey, hobnobbing with Henry King and Charles Pickett and George McKinstry. Sutter once described McKinstry as "all-time the same—full of fun and wit,"[27] a phrase which might be applied to the whole foursome of King, Pickett, McKinstry, and Kern. In a way Ned could see in each of his three friends a bit of what the last two years had meant to him. King, the former effete easterner, had become a trail-hardened expeditioner. Pickett might have been Kern's alter ego—a buoyant personality thoroughly enjoying his rovings. McKinstry was a reminder of those months at Fort Sutter when men with no administrative training or inclinations had carried out a complex job remarkably well. Kern had not only experienced, like King, the western mystery, but returned with a sizeable part of the image captured by brush and sextant. He had had a good time, although the administration of Fort Sutter was the kind of work which he hoped never to have to repeat. For the rest, especially the western sketching and topography, he was ready whenever another chance might come.

In November Ned and King sailed for home through the Golden Gate on the schooner *Commodore Shubrick*. With them on the ship was Antoine Robidoux, trapper, trader, and scout, who had also served Frémont in the conquest. The three men were already acquainted, and the long voyage, during which they could take turns damning fate and the government for making them bear their own expenses home, would bring them closer. But the next time Edward was to see San Francisco eight years later, Henry King would have died not far from Ned's side, Antoine Robidoux would be blind and paralyzed, and the transformation of Yerba Buena would leave him familiar with little more than the sea and the fog.

27. J. Sutter to R. Kern, Jan. 10, 1852, Huntington Library. For Ned's unhappy comments on the trip home see E. Kern to G. McKinstry, Dec., 1847, Calif. State Library.

CHAPTER 3

The San Juans

Ned, carrying a few belongings, strode long-legged down Philadelphia's Filbert Street, along the narrow walk which separated the stone walls of the houses from the cobbles, to number 62. Up the stoop and, after nearly two years, he was home to his house of bachelor brothers. Dick was there to greet him, whooping about the wild Indian just arrived, the young Lochinvar come out of the West. Benjamin was there, and John, whom the younger brothers called "the Old Man" (he was sixteen years older than Edward), probably welcomed him with a handshake. Ned wandered with them through the house—the studio where he and Dick and John had taught drawing, Ben's office with books and medical instruments. Mary, Ned's older sister, would come over later. She lived not far away with her husband, William Wolfe. Ned was devoted to Mary, eighteen years his senior, old enough to be his mother and the head of the clan since the death of the elder Kerns.

Ned was anxious for a long talk with Dick, his closest brother. We can imagine them that first night sharing a bottle, as they had many a time before, and talking into the dawn. Dick was intensely curious. What was this West really like: How wild was a Plains Indian? How savage? Were Catlin's drawings true likenesses? How about squaws in the Rockies? And those rapscallions, the Mexicans! What had happened during the war in California?

Ned and Dick were only two years apart, and at least one of their friends thought there was a striking resemblance.[1] But in contrast with Ned's wiriness, Dick was stocky with rounder cheeks and a little belly that made his coats pull at the buttons. A shock of hair fell carelessly over his forehead; his eyes were soft and relaxed with lines of laughter around them. He blew the flute a little, enjoyed the theater and the poetry of Thomas Hood, and loved to pun. But his frivolous and energetic nature was balanced by serious qualities, all attested by Henry Schoolcraft, the ethnologist —competent draftsmanship, linguistic abilities, and an innate sagacity. Through perseverence and talent he had made a moderate success of the studio since Ned's departure. "Business is good," he wrote his younger brother, "and the income certain; there is sufficient for Old Man and self."[2]

Within the last few months Ned and Dick and Ben had all been elected members of the Philadelphia Academy of

1. G. McKinstry to E. Kern, Dec. 23, 1851, Fort Sutter Papers.
2. The earlier Henry Schoolcraft comment is from his *Indian Tribes, 4,* 597; see a similar statement in *St. Louis Evening News,* Dec. 19, 1853, as quoted in Nolie Mumey, *John Williams Gunnison* (Denver, 1955), p. 130. The R. Kern quote is from R. Kern to E. Kern, Feb. 10, 1847, Fort Sutter Papers. For a student's twelve weeks' course of two lessons a week, a teacher received no more than $25.00 (*Catalogue of 36th Annual Exhibition of Pennsylvania Academy of Fine Arts,* 1859, back cover). But in a time when drawing stood high in the desirable equipment of a young lady or gentleman, students were not hard to find. A few such classes could provide a basic income. William Brandon, *The Men and the Mountain* (New York, 1955), p. 56, believes the above quotation indicates business had not always been as good.

Natural Sciences.[3] It was no inconsiderable recognition, and Ned's inclusion, at least, reflected the way in which the scientific societies of America, growing enormously in the 1840's, drew upon western surveys and expeditions as sources of information. Men like Ned acted as field workers for eastern scientists, and the data they gathered was eagerly sought by the scholarly societies. Since the Philadelphia Academy was one of the oldest, founded in 1812, bales and boxes of specimens, sketches of fauna and fossils, such as those brought back by Kern, were already pouring into its collections and becoming subjects of learned papers in its journals. Most scientists were not specialists, allowing their intellectual curiosities to roam widely and willing to make contributions in a variety of fields. Samuel Morton, for example, member and future president of the Philadelphia Academy and well known to the Kerns, seriously researched the subjects of medicine, geology, and paleontology, as well as zoology and human anatomy. And the West had something to add to all of these disciplines.

During Ned's absence, Dick, as a scientific illustrator, had made numerous contacts with Philadelphia academicians. Joseph Leidy, the anatomist, "one of the most versatile scientists America has ever produced," brought several commissions Dick's way—among them the illustrations in a volume of medical botany for Joseph Carson and a set of drawings in microscopic anatomy for Paul B. Goddard.[4]

3. Richard was elected May 25, 1847; Benjamin, September, 1847; and Edward, October 26, 1847. Venia T. Phillips, Librarian, Academy of Natural Sciences of Philadelphia, to R. Hine, Sept. 4, 1958; see also W. S. W. Ruschenberger, *A Notice of the Origin, Progress and Present Condition of the Academy of Natural Sciences of Philadelphia* (Philadelphia, 1852), pp. 75 f.

4. The description of Leidy is from Ralph Bates, *Scientific Societies in the United States* (New York, 1945), p. 35. The Kern work can be seen in Joseph Carson, *Illustrations of Medical Botany* (2 vols. Philadelphia, 1847) and Paul Goddard, ed., *A System of Human Anatomy* (Philadelphia, 1848); neither of these volumes credits Richard Kern, but in R. Kern to E. Kern, Feb. 10, 1847, Fort Sutter Papers, he is specific about work on these or very similar volumes.

So the two new members of the Philadelphia Academy might pursue over their night lamps a whole set of scientific questions about the West. As a botanist Ned could describe California redwoods, Monterey cypress, the Fremontia, artemisia plains, or the poppy and lupine of the Sacramento; as a zoologist, the prairie dog or the ways of the buffalo; as a geologist, unknown coal formations, passes in the Rockies, and the Great Salt Lake, so impregnated that small bushes blown into its waters became delicate saline crystallizations; as a geographer, the extremes of temperature between desert nights and days or the strange series of parallel ranges in the Great Basin; as an ethnologist, Cheyenne tepees compared with Digger huts or grasshopper mash with acorn gruel. It was not hard to arouse deeper curiosity about the West.

Frémont meanwhile had returned to a reception far different from Ned's—glaring publicity and Army squabbles shrouded in the sectional conflict of North and South and the political machinations of his father-in-law, Thomas Hart Benton. Frémont marched home to a court-martial, charged with mutiny and insubordination. Benton, a jealous scion of a proud family, acted as his lawyer in court, and for nearly three months beginning in November Benton's voice boomed against the entrenched stubbornness of an Army old guard, represented chiefly by Stephen Kearny and the military court. But to no avail. On January 31, 1848, Lieutenant Colonel Frémont was declared guilty of mutiny, of disobedience to a superior officer, and conduct prejudicial to good order.

The effect on Ned must have been devastating. He knew Frémont was honorable. Even with the Mexicans in California he had acted honestly, asking for permission to enter the province and leaving when Castro demanded, to return only for the business of war. Later, to have obeyed Stockton rather than Kearny might have shown poor judgment, but it did not prove mutiny.

President Polk remitted the sentence and ordered Frémont to take his sword and report for active duty. Instead, amid Benton's howls and protestations of innocence, Frémont resigned his commission.

After such humiliation, a proud man seeks to retaliate by renewing his faith in himself and in self-justification. These needs rose quickly in Frémont and centered themselves on California—on a new beginning as far from Eastern politics as the giant Sequoia from the scrub pine of the Atlantic piedmont. In his closing words to the court he had proudly declared that though he had been brought as a prisoner from California, "I could return to it, after this trial is over, without rank or guards," a loved and respected man. On the way to California, to regain his honor and refurbish his fame, he would lead an expedition in the middle of winter across the central Rockies. He and Benton had long shared the hope of proving the central route for a transcontinental railroad, not only to keep the future road away from the slave-ridden South, but to make St. Louis the eastern terminus of the western cornucopia. Such plans rested ultimately on the survey of a route near the 38th parallel and the demonstration that the passes were usable in winter, for a fair-weather railroad would be no better than a fair-weather friend. Army funds were no longer available to Frémont, and Benton failed to get a Congressional appropriation; but St. Louis businessmen were willing to underwrite some of the costs. It would be a careful topographic survey charting passes, measuring snowfall and snowpack, and recording temperatures and gradients. The Frémont fourth expedition was born.

Frémont asked Edward to come along, though unfortunately this time there could be no promise of pay. Perhaps when they got through to California, Congress would recognize their work with retroactive recompense. The prospects of a successful expedition were good: Frémont had discussed the idea carefully with Kit Carson, then in Washington; able men were volunteering. Charles Preuss, engaged in preparing the finished map of the last expedition, now would go on the next, his wife this time be damned. Henry King had signed, in spite of the fact that he was in love and about to be married. Ned needed no urging. He volunteered immediately and before he knew it he had talked Dick and Ben into going too. Ned's recommendation would be sufficient to get his brothers accepted, and, besides, with no salary, places on the expedition came more easily than before. The three Kerns became "the most strenuous advocates" of the expedition.[5] Raphael Proue, one of the French *engagés* of 1845, visited Edward in Philadelphia and bolstered the general enthusiasm.

Sitting in his room on Filbert Street before leaving, Dick waxed Romantic and entered in Mary's album some lines translated from the German:

When to the land where the citron flowers blooming,
The swan speeds his southwardly flight;
When the red of the evening in the far west is sinking
And through the deep woods steal the shadows of night,
Then doth my heart with deep grief complain
That never, ah never shall I see thee again.
Parting, ah parting, parting gives pain.

So to Westport again, but this time it was October. The town that fall was quiet compared with the raucous spring of 1845. There was goldenrod on the prairies rather than spiderwort. The cottonwood leaves were turning and the prairie wind bore a chill. Thirty-six men gathered, most of them Ned's friends from California days, like King and Godey, the latter's sharp senses gauging the wind and predicting a cold winter. Tom Breckenridge was back, a seasoned mountaineer with a Missouri twang. Lorenzo Vin-

---

5. Alexis Godey in New York *Evening Post*, Oct. 30, 1856; reprinted in LeRoy R. and Ann W. Hafen, eds., *Frémont's Fourth Expedition: A Documentary Account* (Glendale, Calif., 1960), p. 272.

centhaler had signed again, probably because it was an inexpensive way to get to California; the Kerns did not like Vincenthaler and their feeling was to sharpen on the trip ahead. There was the usual crew of French *engagés,* led by Raphael Proue, who had served Frémont on all three previous expeditions, and including Vincent Tableau, a redhaired Frenchman whom everyone called Sorrel. For awhile some of the same Delaware Indians that Ned had sketched in 1845 joined them, including Sagundai of the swarthy face and flat nose.

The newcomers, the greenhorns, emphasized the heterogeneous nature of the group. Andrew Cathcart, for example, son of a wealthy Ayrshire family, had come west as a British soldier on leave searching for game and excitement. As Frémont's hunter on this expedition he would find more than enough of both. Dick and Ned sketched his portrait, his mouth almost hidden by moustaches below a sharp, aquiline nose.[6] The scientific corps which included Preuss and the Kerns was supplemented by a botanist, Frederick Creutzfeldt, probably a friend of Preuss. The bulky scientific equipment was again on hand—surveying instruments, cans and kegs and presses for collecting, alcohol for a preservative, but mixed with tartar emetic to prevent its preserving men rather than specimens.

A dawn of late October heard the damn's and the *sacre's* and whoa-a's of the first catching up, and there began the rhythm of shivering predawn breakfasts, unmanageable packs, straying animals, gumbo mud, and night fires. Dick took it all in stride with a smile ("Everything went off well with the exception of some packs on wild mules and they went off too").

Ben started out happily enough, intrigued with fossil

6. Sketch reproduced in Hafen and Hafen, eds., *Frémont's Fourth Expedition,* p. 121. Cf. Preuss, *Exploring with Frémont,* entry of Jan. 31, 1948. Cathcart had come to St. Louis with George Frederick Ruxton before joining Frémont.

shells, rock formations, or milk vetch. But within a short while a darker strain crowded his enthusiasm, and his journal received repeated comments on monotonous, disagreeable country, wistfully compared with the scenery back home.[7] A good part of his dissatisfaction arose from mistreatment. He had been hired as doctor of the expedition, and Ned must have told him that on any such western safari the specialists, particularly doctors, were not subject to the routine chores of camp—did not have to gather wood or saddle mules or stand guard. But on this expedition Frémont felt unusual pressures; although he had a plethora of scientists he was short on laborers, and he had already ordered Ben to guard duty and to jobs with the mules.

Ned, meanwhile, was calloused, inured, enjoying the taste of prickly pear, even beginning to think like a mountain man: "Godey today killed two [buffalo] cows, and we had a glorious mess of guts . . . ."[8] He continued to sketch enthusiastically—the front face of a bull, daily camps, the Kiowas and Arapahoes passing along the Arkansas—and at night he and Dick would draw by the firelight, their tears from the woodsmoke watering the colors.

As members now of the Philadelphia Academy they were sensitive to a wide scientific front. They could make Joseph Leidy happy with word of any new variety of lizard or mouse; Joseph Carson would be pleased to hear of any uncatalogued plants, especially those believed by the Indians to have medicinal properties; Samuel Morton was anxious to get some Indian skulls for comparative purposes. All of the Kerns kept their journals full of scientific descriptions of clouds, flowers, and animals.

7. Cf. entries of Nov. 8, 15, 27, Dec. 9 and 13, 1848, B. Kern, Diary, 1848–49, Huntington Library.

8. E. Kern, Diary, Oct. 31, 1848, Huntington Library. Unless otherwise noted, subsequent quotations in this chapter from Edward, Richard, or Benjamin are from their diaries for this expedition in the Huntington Library. Cf. LeRoy R. and Ann W. Hafen, eds., *Frémont's Fourth Expedition: A Documentary Account* (Glendale, Calif., 1960).

They had no guide for the Rockies when they left West-port. Frémont, as was customary, hoped to find in the few settlements on the eastern fringe of the mountains some toughened trapper to lead them through the maze of passes and canyons, much as they had used Bill Williams in 1845. At the tattered hamlet of Pueblo they were lucky to find Williams again. He was willing to join them, to mount his mule, to set his wrinkled face toward the mountains he had tramped for two decades. No one knew the passes better. If they met Indians, most likely Utes, their guide would be a blood brother of that tribe. For their purposes it would have been hard to find the equal of their old friend Bill Williams.

Williams joined Godey in predicting a hard winter. And sure enough, as early as November 3 they ran into driving snow, and when they reached the Arkansas River, the current already bore chunks of ice. Ned and Henry King, nevertheless, stood by the numbing water at sunset and bathed. At Pueblo they heard reports of deep snow in the mountains, and thereafter worriedly watched the Spanish Peaks, which the Indians called the Breasts of the World, rising nakedly before them, frigidly white. As they crossed the Antoine Robidoux gap in the Sangre de Cristo Range, Dick described the men as looking "like old Time or Winter—icicles an inch long were pendant from our moustache & beard."

Beyond the Sangre de Cristos lay the high valley where the headwaters of the Rio Grande collect and empty southward toward Taos and Santa Fe.[9] Across the river rose the white spine of the Rockies, here called the San Juan Range, whose sprawling snow pack, like an ice wall athwart the continental divide, formed the chief challenge for the ex-

---

9. Four years later Gwinn Harris Heap, having tramped this valley in the kinder month of June, yet described it as "difficult and dangerous on account of the numerous sloughs and marshes." *Central Route to the Pacific* (Philadelphia, 1854), p. 35.

pedition. Even before the assault, Ben Kern wrote, "All
very tired." As the file of thirty-three men with their mules
wound across the valley into the higher canyons, snow
reached the level of a mounted man's elbow. *(Fig. 16)* Ben's
stockings froze so hard they had to be shaved off. "Prospects," he said, "becoming somewhat gloomy."

Frémont's determination remained as steel. Ahead in that
"great dark barrier" of storm clouds perhaps he imagined
the face of Stephen Watts Kearny or a circle of Army judges;
and in the distant thunder, the condescending voice of the
President in his pardon. He must conquer the others by
conquering this. The men battled on; there was little
grumbling. And Ned with his infectious respect would have
agreed with an earlier comment of Kit Carson's, that for
Frémont nothing was impossible.[10]

Doubts, however, were arising. One terribly important
question was the route over the San Juans. Someone later
saw an entry in Bill Williams' notebook which read, "I
wanted to go one way and Frémont will go another, and
right here our troubles will commence."[11] Tom Breckenridge, who was sharing blankets with Old Bill at the time,
maintained that the guide wanted either to go north over
the Cochetopa Pass or turn south around the San Juans,
but that Frémont insisted on heading more directly west,
sticking close to the 38th parallel. As Dick said, "with the
wilfully blind eyes of rashness and self-conceit and confidence he pushed on."[12]

So they stayed along the 38th parallel. Winds sliced into
their marrow. Mules began to drop. Without the beasts

---

10. Grant, ed., *Kit Carson's Own Story*, p. 66. Cf. Thomas E. Breckenridge, "The Story of a Famous Expedition," *Cosmopolitan, 21* (1896), 401.

11. McGehee Papers, as quoted in Favour, *Old Bill Williams*, p. 158. Cf.
"Extracts from Journal of Lt. J. H. Simpson," MS. 126, Fort Sutter Papers.

12. Breckenridge, "Story," pp. 401, 402. For the Dick Kern quote see his
Journal as quoted in Quincy (Ill.) *Journal*, reprinted in Philadelphia *Eve-
ning Bulletin*, June 2, 1849; see also LeRoy R. and Ann W. Hafen, eds.,
Frémont's Fourth Expedition, p. 265, for a different printing of same quote.

and their packs the men were done for, and sustaining the animals thus assumed first priority. But with fodder gone, the mules would one by one stop, tremble, fall, and die.

The men fared little better. They were nearing twelve thousand feet altitude, which they could feel in every weakened step. Their noses bled. "Some became stupid from the cold." In the third week of December, "days of horror, desolation, despair and almost continued heavy winds, intense cold and snow storms, we laid in camp, fluctuating between hope and despair. Half erected the tent and built a fire in front. One after the other became smoke blind and sat under the drippings from the tent . . . backs covered with the drifty snow, a situation making it a misery to exist."

For five days, just beyond the summit in a little clump of pine and fir, the outer storm and the inner fatigue completely stalled them. Ben peeped out from eight inches of snow on his blanket and told Dick the expedition was destroyed; they would be lucky to get out with their lives. Frémont likewise understood: "We were overtaken by sudden and inevitable ruin."[13] Almost too late, with some of his hot determination frozen like the mules on that San Juan ridge, Frémont ordered a retreat.

They called the grove beyond the crest "Camp Dismal" and the place to which they now returned "Camp Hope."

On Christmas Day the weather cleared, though still bone-cracking with cold. Frémont ordered all baggage carried back to the camp on the Rio Grande, and Christmas morning the Kerns, their sixty- and seventy-pound packs bulky with surgical instruments, medicines, drawing paper and water colors, made two trips to the top of the hill to bring up their equipment. That evening Camp Hope had a Christmas dinner. Godey acted as chef. He cooked some hoarded elk meat into a stew, boiled a handful of rice and brewed coffee. For toasting the season there was even a lit-

13. B. Kern to "Joe," Feb. 20, 1849, Huntington Library; John Frémont to Jessie Frémont, Jan. 27, 1849, reprinted in Bigelow, *Frémont*, p. 368.

tle alcohol, "hot stuff" to Dick. After the days of starvation rations, Ben was made sick by the meal and he vomited all night.

As the expedition slipped back toward the valley, it broke into segments like a frayed rope. On New Year's Eve the Kern section consisted of the three brothers; the Scot, Andrew Cathcart; and two Indian boys. They were about three miles behind the main body. They still had strength enough to sing a few songs around the fire that night, and Dick read aloud from Thomas Hood while "Ned minced boild mule meat for pies for tomorrows New Years treat." The alcohol was gone, but they fired their guns to salute the New Year, and Dick's spirits were high enough to call it "the pleasantest night since our start."

Actually their situation was desperate. On the day after Christmas Frémont had dispatched four men—his trusted Henry King, Old Bill as guide, Tom Breckenridge, and Frederick Creutzfeldt, the botanist—to hurry on for help, as far as Taos or Abiquiu if necessary. Between the expedition and shelter lay at least 130 miles, perhaps 160, of winter-clamped wilds over which the main party, in its weak state, could average only about five miles a day. Their food supplies, except for the dying mules, were all but gone, and game had moved to lower, sheltered valleys. On January 3, as the Kerns analyzed their baggage for what should be left behind, Ben saw Ned, dispirited, "sitting in gloom by the fire"; Doc, himself "a weakly and melancholy object," tried to cheer Ned up. Later, by a mockingly bright moon, Ben thought he saw several mice, and longed for a mouse trap, this time hoping to eat rather than preserve the specimens.

The first man to die was Raphael Proue, the hardy Frenchman who had shared, in Philadelphia, the Kern enthusiasm for the expedition. The second was Henry King, who gave out as he and his relief party foundered in the valley drifts. Ned later heard the news of his old comrade's death along with rumors that the survivors, like the Donner

Party, had fed on the body. During January Proue and King were followed by eight others—ten in all, almost one-third of the company. In this extremity Ned came to look on death "with as little sympathy as I would have done had they been dogs. 'Twill be my turn soon, poor fellow he has but a few hours start of me, or he was a good man,' were all the words of sympathy that were expressed."[14]

On January 11 Frémont, despairing of King's relief party, set out with Alex Godey and three others for help. Lorenzo Vincenthaler, who was left in charge of the remaining twenty-four men, became the victim of suspicions breeding in minds robbed of nourishment, until on the twenty-first he resigned "all command of the party, declared it broken up and said each one must take care of himself." A group of the strongest went on ahead; the weakest—the three Kerns, Cathcart, and five others—stayed behind and swore to stick together. To Ned's mind, "here commenced our severest suffering." For a few days they made some progress using the ice of the Rio Grande for a path. "Over its congealed surface a somber shade was cast by the overhanging trees covered with long white frost which hung like a thick fringe from their barren boughs."[15]

Finally they bogged down completely. Dick, no puns left, wrote simply, "these were days of Misery, and death would soon have ended them." Ned wrote his will, and for six days they sank into a listless stupor. Then on January 28, sitting dumbly around their fire, they slowly caught the sound of a distant halloo. One of them rose weakly and said, "Christ, there's a man on horseback over the river." Someone else murmured, "Relief, by Heaven," and with punished lungs they all yelled. Alex Godey, himself worn

14. E. Kern to Mary Wolfe, [late Feb. or early March], 1849, Huntington Library.

15. E. Kern to Mary Wolfe, Feb. 10, 1849, Huntington Library. The description of the river is from Micajah McGehee, "Rough Times in Rough Places," *Century, 41* (1891), 775. McGehee had passed only a few days earlier.

and haggard, rode over, saying "damned glad to find you alive." Some were so snow blind they thought it was Frémont and weakly saluted. Godey brought bread and meat; ". . . we cried and some of us trembled with joy at the sight of it."[16]

So ended their ordeal, their racking tour through the environs of death which left them all changed men. When they finally reached Taos, they found Frémont, too, a disturbed man, anxious "to leave this country, and all thoughts and all things connected with recent events." On February 13, after two weeks of rest at Kit Carson's house, making loans and buying fresh animals and supplies, he led the battered but re-equipped expedition out of the Taos adobes on the Gila route to the west. Behind him remained six bitter men, refusing to continue—Bill Williams, Andrew Cathcart, Joe Stepperfeldt, and the three Kerns—"some who preferred to go among strangers awhile," Jessie, Frémont's wife, later euphemistically described them, "until the scenes in which they had been actors, had become dimmed by time." Before the year was out Frémont rationalized the debacle of the fourth expedition into success. "The result was entirely satisfactory. It convinced me that neither the snow of winter nor the mountain ranges were obstacles in the way of the [rail]road."[17]

The result for the Kerns was anything but satisfactory. For one thing their admiration of Frémont had cracked like spring ice, leaving sharp, jagged disillusionment. Ned held Frémont responsible for abandoning his exhausted men, for leaving the inept Vincenthaler in charge, for failing to return himself to their relief when he could, for

16. The details of the reunion are from R. Kern, Diary; E. Kern to Mary Wolfe, Feb. 10, 1849; McGehee, "Rough Times," p. 777; and B. Kern to "Joe," Feb. 20, 1849.

17. Quotations in order within paragraph: John Frémont to Jessie Frémont, Feb. 6, 1849, in Bigelow, *Frémont,* p. 373; Jessie Frémont, "Great Events," Nevins Collection, Bancroft Library; John Frémont to Snyder, Dec. 11, 1849, in Bigelow, *Frémont,* p. 391.

taking all of the supplies when he left for California, rather than sharing with the almost destitute men who stayed behind.[18] But the deepest split came over the assessment of blame.

The Kerns were willing to admit that Old Bill Williams had probably lost his way. Ned wrote to his friend Antoine Robidoux in Missouri, still suffering the effects of his California wound, that Williams' route "was evidently mistaken, for a worse road I never saw."[19] But even this letter left open the possibility that Williams was only trying to work out a trail under orders with which he disagreed—so the Kerns came to believe. Williams, they were sure, would have skirted the 38th parallel route, but Frémont held the expedition to it.

Ned soon learned that Frémont was publicly censuring Old Bill Williams without himself assuming a particle of guilt. "The error of our journey," Frémont said, "was committed in engaging this man [Williams]," and Frémont's father-in-law echoed the sentiments by labeling the guide a "passport to disaster."[20] Frémont belatedly intimated that Williams had designs on the property of the expedition, that his mind was unsound, and that "in starving times no man who knew him ever walked in front of Bill Williams."[21]

Such self-righteousness and prevarication left the Kerns furious. They had huddled around too many campfires with Old Bill, had faced death with him and nearly starved with him without ever fearing him. They might have been even angrier had they heard Frémont's backhanded snipes at the

18. Cf. R. Kern's remarks of March 19, 1849, copied from Quincy (Ill.) *Journal*, in Philadelphia *Evening Bulletin*, June 2, 1849.

19. E. Kern to A. Robidoux, Feb. 11, 1849, in Nevins, *Frémont* (1939), p. 628.

20. John Frémont to Jessie Frémont, Jan. 27, 1849, in Bigelow, *Frémont*, p. 367; Thomas H. Benton, *Thirty Years' View*, 2 (2 vols. New York, 1854), 719.

21. Jessie Frémont, "Great Events," pp. 93, 84.

bravery of his men in general. Their courage failed, he told his wife, "in fact, I have never seen men so soon discouraged by misfortune as we were on this occasion; but, as you know, the party was not constituted like the former ones." Proue was made out to have died solely from lack of nerve: "In a sunshiny day, and having with him means to make a fire, he threw his blankets down in the trail and laid there till he froze to death."[22]

One hour after Ned arrived exhausted in Taos, he began a long letter in a tired scrawl to his sister Mary. He had heard that a caravan left in the early morning for the states. He knew that his family must be worried, so, postponing the luxury of a bed, he wrote till midnight. What he called a "general outline of our miseries" covered eight pages and clearly revealed his intention to quit the expedition.[23]

Some weeks later he wrote Mary again. This time it was a careful message with an elaborately illuminated first page of latticed initials, serpents entwining skulls, and a pen drawing of Proue's death. *(Fig. 17)* By the second sentence he was unleashing his fury at Frémont: "he has broken faith with all of us."

Dick and I were to have accompanied him as artists and Doc. as Medico and Naturalist. When out we found our situation suddenly changed from what we had started for to that of mulateers each with his number of packs and whatever work in his particular branch might turn up besides. This you must believe was somewhat cutting to our dignity—not that any of us were unwilling to assist in any work *if necessity* required it—but this was not the case. You know too that flattery is certainly not apart of any Kern more particularly of Dicks or Bens. So that was a damper on their

22. John Frémont to Jessie Frémont, Jan. 27, 1849, in Bigelow, *Frémont,* pp. 368, 369; Jessie Frémont, "Great Events," p. 86.
23. E. Kern to Mary Wolfe, Feb. 10, 1849, Huntington Library.

prospects. Natures more illy suited [i.e., Dick and Ben with Frémont] could not well have been thrown together. This is the principal reason on the part of F. (who loves to be told of his greatness) . . . . Another amiable weakness he has, that of believing the reports of the meanest in his camp. Hardly one time has he treated us with the respect due our situation or ourselves, and jealous of anyone who may know as much or more of any subject than himself (for he delights to associate among those who *should* be his inferiors—which may in some measure account for the reputation he has gained of being, for a man of his tallents so excessively modest. A thing by the by which many adopt to hide their want of depth.) he very naturally begat a dislike to Doc. and took no small pleasure at showing it to others, with whom good sense and the behavior belonging to the character of a gentleman should have forbidden him holding converse on such subjects.[24]

Of course, Ben had been unhappy from early in the trip. His sourness must have immediately antagonized Frémont, who, after his humiliation in the court-martial, craved encouragement and enthusiasm more than at any other time in his life. If, as Ned said, he came to dislike Doc and gave him the unpleasant jobs of night duty and mule packing, from which as doctor he should have been exempt, Ned and Dick naturally would have sprung straightway to the defense of their elder brother. Frémont, himself upset by the trial, in this situation found Ned, conscious of a respected brother's ill-treatment, changed, too, from the person he had known in California.[25]

24. E. Kern to Mary Wolfe [late Feb. or early March], 1849, Huntington Library.

25. On the other hand, none of these unsavory comments on Frémont (except the simple fact that Ben took guard duty) appears in the daily diaries of any of the three brothers, nor does Ned intimate such ideas in his first letter to Mary. There is a possibility that Ned during his enforced leisure, seeing events in retrospect, was constructing and believing a stronger case against Frémont than was strictly warranted.

In Taos, however, the immediate problem for the Kerns was how to get home. All their possessions—clothes, surgical instruments, medicines, drawing equipment, sketches, bird and plant collections, perhaps even a little money—remained cached along the frozen upper waters of the Rio Grande. Nearly flat broke, as Ned said, they could not easily get back to Philadelphia without retrieving that abandoned dunnage.[26] As the weeks went by, the danger of someone pilfering the cache increased. So later in February, though the snows had melted but little, Old Bill and Ben Kern, with a few Mexican helpers, started back up the Rio Grande. That Ben went instead of Ned or Dick was probably a comment on Ben's special eagerness to get home.

The drifts still lay deep, but this time they themselves were fed and rested. They quickly located the main cache, packed, and by March 14 were ready to return.

Meanwhile from Taos young Lieutenant Joseph Whittlesey and a small detachment advanced north along the river with orders to seek and chastise the Utes for recent outrages. On March 13 they surprised a Ute camp of fifty lodges in a piñon grove, attacked and killed ten men and about twenty horses, and drove the remaining Indians like chickens in all directions through the snow.[27]

Twelve of these refugees, burning with rage, stumbled late that night or early next morning on a wizened scout and

26. Before he left, Frémont sent one party back for the baggage, but they had failed (John Frémont to T. Benton, Feb. 24, 1849, in Bigelow, *Frémont*, p. 377). Then, in his hurry to leave, he engaged "Uncle Dick" Wootton to fetch the material when the weather permitted. But, after Frémont left, Wootton talked with Old Bill Williams, who explained that the property belonged partly to the Kern boys and himself and they were prepared to go after it. As Wootton put it, "The five former members of the party, who had remained behind, laid claim to all the valuables which I had been promised as compensation for making the trip, and I came to the conclusion that they might go after the stuff themselves." (Richens Lacy Wootton, *"Uncle Dick" Wootton,* as told to Howard L. Conard [Chicago, 1890; reprint Columbus, 1950], p. 200.)

27. Lt. J. H. Whittlesey to Maj. B. L. Beall, March 15, 1849, Old Army Branch, National Archives; Santa Fe *Weekly Gazette,* March 12, 1853.

a whiter white man camped by the river with heavily packed mules. The spirit of revenge had come sweetly soon.

So died Benjamin Kern—in a valley where torment was a fresh memory—and Bill Williams, blood brother by adoption of the men who killed him. The Utes later told an old companion of Bill's that they had not recognized Williams in time and that when they did, they "gave him a chief's burial, mourning for him as for one of their own."[28] Ben's thin body would have shared no such ritual.

A few days earlier in Taos Ned had written his sister, "Doc has returned to the mountains to try to recover some of our lost property, with what success is uncertain. We are anxiously awaiting his return, to move eastward."[29]

28. W. T. Hamilton, *My Sixty Years on the Plains* (New York, 1905), p. 196.
29. E. Kern to Mary Wolfe [late Feb. or early March], 1849, Huntington Library.

20. Richard Kern, *Hos-ta (the Lightning)*. Water color, ca. 9½″ × 5¾″. Academy of Natural Sciences of Philadelphia. Compare lithograph in Simpson, *Navajo Journal* (1850).

21. Edward Kern, *You-pel-lay, or the Green Corn Dance of the Jemez Indians*, 1849. Water color, ca. 5¾" × 9½". Academy of Sciences of Philadelphia. Compare lithograph in Simpson, *Navajo Journal* (1850), where it is erroneously attributed to Richard Kern.

22. Richard Kern, *Navajo Costume.* Lithograph. Simpson, *Navajo Journal* (1850).

23. Richard Kern, *North West View of the Ruins of the Pueblo Pintado in the Valley of the Chaco*, 1849. Water color, ca. 5¾" × 9½". Academy of Natural Sciences of Philadelphia.

24. Richard Kern, *North West View of the Ruins of the Pueblo Pintado in the Valley of the Chaco*. Lithograph. Simpson, *Navajo Journal* (1850).

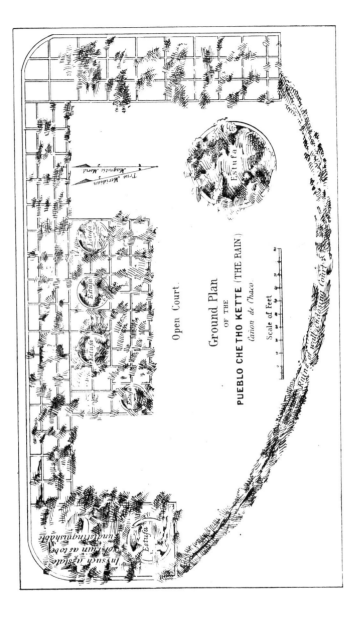

25. Richard Kern, *Ground Plan of the Pueblo Chetho Kette [Chetro Kettle], Cañon de Chaco*. Lithograph. Simpson, *Navajo Journal* (1850).

26. Richard Kern, *Ruins of an Old Pueblo in the Cañón of Chelly* [*White House*], 1849. Water color, ca. 9½″ × 5¾″. Academy of Natural Sciences of Philadelphia.

27. Lithograph of Figure 26. Simpson, *Navajo Journal* (1850).

28. Modern photograph of scene shown in Figure 26. Dr. David DeHarport, Harvard University.

Richard Kern, *Laguna* [*Pueblo*], 1849 (1851?). Wash drawing, 5¾″ × 7¼″. Peabody Museum, Harvard University.

Seth Eastman, engraved version of Figure 29. Schoolcraft, *Indian Tribes* (1851–57), 4.

31. Richard Kern, *Interior of an Estufa at Jemez*, 1849. Pencil sketch, 7¼″ × 9¾″. Peabody Museum, Harvard University.

32. Richard Kern, *Estufa or Council Chamber at Jemez*, 1849. Wash drawing, 7″ × 9⅛″. Peabody Museum, Harvard University.

33. Seth Eastman, engraved version of Figure 32. Schoolcraft, *Indian Tribes* (1851–57), 4.

Map 1. Edward Kern, map of the Navajo Expedition under Lieutenant James H.
Simpson, 1849. Simpson, *Report* (1850).

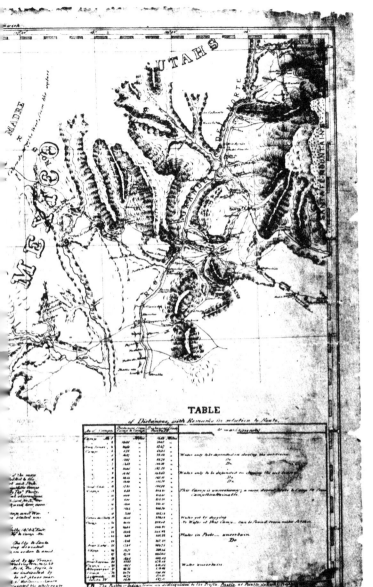

TABLE

of Distances, with Remarks in relation to Route.

Map 2. Richard Kern, map of the Zuñi Expedition under Lieutenant Lorenzo Sitgreaves, 1851. Sitgreaves, *Report* (1853).

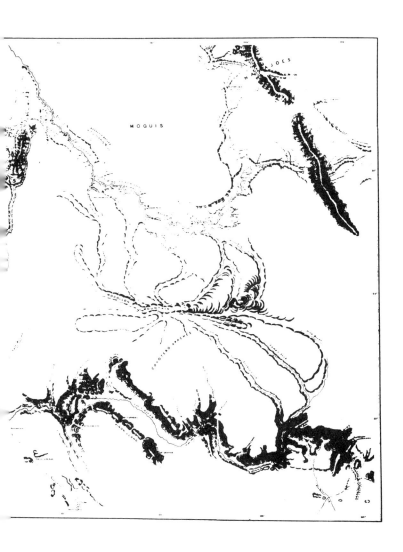

34. Richard Kern, *Indian Blacksmith Shop, Pueblo Zuñi*, 1851. Lithograph. Sitgreaves, *Re* (1853).

35. Richard Kern, *Indian Weaving, Pueblo Zuñi*, 1851. Lithograph. Sitgreaves, *Report* (1853).

CHAPTER 4

New Mexico

When the Kerns were discouraged, one word appeared over and over like a leitmotif in their journals and letters: "gloomy." During the spring of 1849 Ned and Dick gave the word plenty of use. By April they realized that Ben must have been murdered, somewhere under that droning March wind. But they could not go home until they had at least tried to find his body. Isaac Cooper, writing his account of the Frémont third expedition, had quoted from the Ossianic poems, "It is night, I am alone, forlorn on the hill of storms." The same Romantic feeling of a dreary wilderness now gripped the Kerns, and Ned may have recalled the lines he had written in Mary's album before they left home:

> Alas! it is delusion all,
> The future cheats us from afar,
> Nor can we be what we recall,
> Nor dare we think on what we are.

They had no money. "The clothes we have on our back

is all we have saved."[1] Cathcart on leaving for England had
advanced them fifty dollars for sketches he wanted, but
fifty dollars did not last long in price-inflated New Mexico.

They had no plans, except for a negative one: whatever
else, Ned was not going to "butt another mountain this winter anyhow." But in a less wry mood he confided, "I have
lost a start that I never expect to recover again."[2] What he
had lost was not an irrecoverable start but his enchantment
with Frémont, his dependence on his first teacher. The apprentice had seen his master's feet of clay and, his emotional
eyesight intensified by his years of excessive admiration,
now saw the feet as incredibly gross and the clay increasingly
coarse. The master had given the apprentice a great deal—
topographical training, confidence, skills of the trail—but
he could give no more. The indenture was over. Ned was
now strictly on his own; the agony in the San Juans, like
a spiritual torment, had left him free.

A good deal of the bitterness toward Frémont was stirred
by the Kerns' own predicament. Week after discouraging
week, efforts to recover Ben's body came to naught. Sal-
vaging the lost belongings was no more successful.[3]
Through the months and into later years these personal
losses of both brother and baggage, plus the time for hind-
sight, catalyzed the Kern disillusionment with Frémont into
a hatred which blazed forth like the zeal of a convert.

1. E. Kern to Mary Wolfe, Feb. 10, 1849, Huntington Library.
2. The first quote is from E. Kern to Mary Wolfe, Feb. 10, 1849; the
second, from E. Kern to Mary Wolfe [late Feb. or early March], 1849, Huntington Library.
3. The chief hope for recovery of the body came through small detach-
ments of the Army working out of Taos, Abiquiu, or Santa Fe. There is
much correspondence between the Kerns and various Army officers, as well
as with James S. Calhoun, the Indian agent. See Fort Sutter Papers MSS.
127–29; James S. Calhoun, *Official Correspondence*, ed. Annie H. Abel
(Washington, 1915), p. 77. Whether the existing Fort Sutter Papers were a
part of the lost belongings, and thereafter recovered, is a moot point, but I
would agree with Brandon, *The Men and the Mountain*, p. 295, and Helen
Wolfe to Herman Spindt, La Jolla, Calif. (n.d.), Bancroft Library, that they
were not.

Ned and Dick took delight in collecting anti-Frémont ammunition. They wrote Cathcart for an estimate of how much it had cost him to be abandoned in Taos. They searched for testimonials to Old Bill Williams' character. They wrote Charles Pickett details on which he based his later vitriolic political tirades against Frémont. In Taos and Santa Fe they became the center of an anti-Frémont circle, including Joe Stepperfeldt, who sent condemnations to his home-town newspaper; George Reed of the Quartermaster Corps, who reported he had seen Bill Williams' notebook which proved Frémont's primary responsibility for the disaster; and Henry Casey of the commissary at Taos, who recapitulated Frémont's uncivil dealings over supplies. "Old Man" John wrote from Philadelphia that Frémont was apparently not forwarding packages, and that in California he was refusing to see any Philadelphian who admitted knowing the Kerns. There were even stories that he had deliberately destroyed Henry King's diary of the expedition.[4]

Taos for them had certain drawbacks. They had rented a single room, a stable as Ned called it, with dirt floor and a simple door through which donkeys and pigs occasionally poked heads. Ned did the cooking, coaxing their taste buds around to accepting the flavor of chili and tortilla. From his California days he remembered enough Spanish for their needs. But they hungered so much for the gardens of home that they wrote their brother John for some flower seeds. (He sent them larkspur.) Yet there were compensations— the peculiar beauty of tamarisk against a limed adobe, new corn sprouting bright around the dusty pueblo terraces, fandangos, flowing *aguardiente,* the fellowship of Estis'

4. The paragraph's references are in the following order: Philadelphia *Evening Bulletin,* June 2, 1849, quoting from Quincy (Ill.) *Journal;* Helen Wolfe, "Some Kern Notes"; Favour, *Old Bill Williams,* p. 158; "Extracts from Journal of Lt. J. H. Simpson," MS. 126, Fort Sutter Papers; John Kern to R. and E. Kern, May 30–31, 1850, Huntington Library.

Tavern, and perhaps even a señorita or two, who with cig-
arettes "between coral lips, perpetrate winning smiles."[5]

They were in a foreign country, in spite of the fact that
their own flag flew and their own Army ruled. Only a
handful of men from the States, mostly traders and soldiers,
lived in the province. The war was still clear in the collec-
tive mind. The Army was still in command. Mexicans and
Indians still mistrusted the intent of their new governors,
the implications of their new citizenship. It was an exciting
period, full of questions and the setting of precedents. And
the same deep curiosity which first led Ned west now
worked to hold his fascination in this foreign corner.

In the early summer of 1849 Ned and Dick hiked the
sixty miles from Taos to the capital of the territory. Though
the Santa Fe they found was a city of six thousand people, it
was still no more than "a tawny adobe town with a few
green trees, set in a half-circle of carnelian-colored hills,
that and no more." Its one-story adobes were not whitewashed as in Taos, and a contemporary of the Kerns called
the town an extensive brickyard.[6] Here and there like desert
buttes rose the six Catholic churches. Dick sketched the
town from the surrounding hills, giving the buildings less
Spanish feeling than they actually had, injecting a bit too
much of Yankee neatness into the scene, as if the newly
constructed army fort had been able thus rapidly to change
three hundred years of Spanish–Mexican character. *(Fig. 15)*

About the same time the Kerns arrived in Santa Fe, a
young Lieutenant James Hervey Simpson of the Topographical Corps marched in with Captain Randolph Marcy
leading a band of emigrants from Fort Smith, Arkansas.
Lieutenant Simpson, a religious man, was cognizant of his

5. Lewis Garrard, *Wah-to-yah and the Taos Trail,* ed. Ralph Bieber
(Glendale, Calif., 1938), pp. 238, 259.

6. The quotation is from Willa Cather, *Death Comes for the Archbishop*
(Mod. Lib. ed. New York, 1927), p. 271; the "brickyard" reference from
John T. Hughes in William Connelley, *Doniphan's Expedition* (Topeka,
Kan., 1907), p. 215.

duty to "search the land," but he could not conceal his feelings for the new province. New Mexico seemed to him naked and barren. He loathed its drab colors, chili and tortillas nauseated him, and he was certain that the only food the Mexicans could not ruin was the boiled chicken egg.

He found waiting new orders from Washington. Rather than proceed with Marcy to California, he was to stop in this wasteland and without delay send to the Topographical Bureau a report on his route from Fort Smith to Santa Fe, including full details of its military and commercial possibilities and its facilities in wood, grass, and water. To do this he urgently needed trained assistants to help with the illustrations and the map. What a coincidence that two of Frémont's best draughtsmen were stranded, unemployed, in Santa Fe—gifts from his guardian angel!

Through five weeks of July and early August the three worked steadily. Simpson had left Washington under the assumption that he would return there to prepare his report; he had consequently brought none of the proper pens, papers, and instruments to process and plot his observations. The Kern drawing equipment lay stained and rusting in the mountain rains. So they ransacked every supply in Santa Fe, Simpson requisitioned the corps in Washington, and Ned wrote hurriedly to his brother John to send pens and paper and India ink. The supplies came, of course, too late, after the work had gone to Washington on all sorts of papers, done with all kinds of improper pens. In these weeks, however, Simpson had grown to respect his aides: "these gentlemen had learned what a practical acquaintance with life, in its more destitute forms, will always develop— a ready resort to, and application of, expedients . . . ."[7]

7. James H. Simpson, *Journal of a Military Reconnaissance from Santa Fe, New Mexico, to the Navajo Country . . . in 1849* (Philadelphia, 1852), p. 4; hereafter cited as Simpson, *Navajo Journal*. Cf. Fort Sutter Papers, MSS 155–57.

In his quiet way, working with Dick and with Simpson, getting to know the Army officers, becoming a part of the small Anglo–American community in Santa Fe, Ned came to see that conditions here were not far different from those he had known in California. New Mexico, like California, was a collection of partly resentful, partly grateful Mexicans, a few friendly Indian tribes, and a larger number of hostile ones. Here, however, the Apaches and Navajos had systematized their hostility into a long tradition of raid and retaliation without much interference from the Mexican government. It was not simply white against red, however, for the Pueblo Indians had long sided with the Mexican against their age-old Navajo enemy. When the American Army came, it assumed the job of protecting each against the other and, chiefly because its handful of troops was ineffectively concentrated within rather than at the approaches to the towns, ended with the hostility of all. The Navajo and Apache were coming to realize that the arm of the United States government, like that of the Mexican, was a brittle reed.

Colonel John M. Washington, military and civil governor of the territory, was determined to effect changes. He presented the raiders with the same alternative which the white men had been offering the Indian from the beginning, "cultivate the earth for an honest livelihood, or be destroyed."[8] As if in response, the Navajo and Apache aggressions that spring, the traditional season for breaking treaties, were worse than the year before. Colonel Washington's answer was a major punitive expedition into the heart of the raiders' own country.

His goal was deep in what is now the huge Navajo Reservation, if necessary even as far as the Canyon de Chelly. He gathered a force of over 350—four companies of infantry with pack mules; artillery including a six-pounder; several

8. John M. Washington, *Letters* (31st Cong., 1st Sess., Hs. Ex. Doc. 5, Pt. 1), p. 105.

companies of Mexican volunteers, who spent most of their time deserting; a band of friendly Pueblo Indians, who made excellent picket-guards, waiting stoically each evening around the colonel's tent for instructions; plus a crew of specialized agents and interpreters. Such an army moving through unmapped, hostile country needed expert guidance. And the officers knew well that this would not be the last time they would be called into this forbidding task; the careful mapping and surveying of the area could be of great future value. They therefore commandeered the two Kern brothers and Lieutenant Simpson to orient the movements of this punitive army and to measure with the white man's nineteenth-century instruments the cubits of an untamed land.

Ned and Dick in August rendezvoused with the Army at the pueblo of Jemez, and there amid Indian dances and intriguing pueblo adobes Simpson and the Kerns began one of the first scientific records of white penetration into the Navajo country—a land of angular canyons, red mesas, and unexplored ruins. For men of such curiosity it was an exciting assignment. They crowded their journals with esoteric Indian customs and myths which even the Indians had half forgotten. For this lore they relied heavily upon Hosta, a handsome, intelligent Indian governor of the Jemez Pueblo, who accompanied the expedition. (*Figs. 19 and 20*) Hosta would take them, for example, into a kiva, explaining symbols like the white and the forked lightning or rituals like the worship of the Sun, who governs the world. Dick would sketch the figures on the walls while Ned or Simpson jotted down Hosta's rich words: "Sing in the Spring for Montezuma to bring them rain . . . and when the Sun comes in the morning he puts away the children of the night."[9]

The 1849 expedition was unlike anything Ned had ever experienced with Frémont, when a tightly knit group

9. R. Kern, Journal, 1849, entries ff. Aug. 19. Cf. Simpson, *Navajo Journal*, p. 21.

worked almost by unwritten code. Now the Kerns marched with a ponderous hulk of an army in which discipline was strict and desertions were frequent. The Kerns and Simpson consequently kept to themselves and quietly did their own work. They were, after all, the scientists of the expedition, and their interests were far from the punitive aims of the regular Army. They felt lucky to be along: how many men did they know at the Academy in Philadelphia who would give their souls to be thus observing Pueblos and Navajos in their native habitat! Moreover, in the days ahead they could measure a few skulls for Morton; snare some strange lizards for Leidy; and capture for their own delight any number of bright birds from a *terra incognita*.

In this sense Simpson, with wide scientific curiosity, made an excellent companion. And a mutual dislike of Frémont also held the three men together. Simpson had begun collecting data about Frémont's fourth expedition, and he let Ned copy entries from his private diary, including an affirmation by John Hatcher, a trapper friend of Williams, that Old Bill could not possibly have led Frémont wrong, and a secondhand story from John Scott, Frémont's hunter, saying Frémont deliberately overruled Williams in choice of passes.[10]

Perhaps Simpson's feeling for Frémont's unrighteousness was an indication of his own deep religious sense, a sense foreign to any Kern. (It is hard to imagine Ned describing an abandoned church at Jemez in Simpson's way, "How amiable are thy tabernacles, O Lord of Hosts.") In Biblical fashion Simpson concluded that the surrounding barrenness was divine retribution on a wicked native people. Not long after he wrote this, they saw, lonely on the Rio Chaco ahead, like a materialization of the tumbled walls of Jericho, the expedition's first view of an ancient ruin, Pueblo Pintado. *(Figs. 23 and 24)*

10. "Extracts from Journal of Lt. J. H. Simpson," MS. 126, Fort Sutter Papers.

It was among the first of their brushes with the antiqui-
ties of the Southwest, those crumbling remains of a vanished
culture which have so puzzled beholders of the dry deserts
from the Spaniards on. American traders like Josiah Gregg
had described a few of them in print: "built of slabs of fine-
grit sand-stone . . . these structures are very massive and
spacious."[11] But it was left to the Kerns and Simpson to
awaken the American people to the significance and com-
plexity of these monuments.

At Pintado the three artist–scientists, almost forgetting
the Army, became archaeologists. They described with excitement the masonry "resembling mosaic work," the gray
sandstone with its reddish tinge, the ground-plan measure-
ments and compass directions, the number of rooms and
stories, architectural details, including the absence of the
curved arch, and the red and black designs of the glazed
shards. Expressing an aroused Romantic sense, Dick wrote
in his journal, "The wolfe and lizard and hare are the only
inhabitants and the bright wild flowers fill the open court
and halls. Who built it no one knows."

Pintado lay on the threshold of an entire canyon of ruins,
called Chaco, and to explore it Dick and Simpson, with
guide and escort, left the main body of troops; the Army
deprived Ned of the adventure by ordering him to continue
his daily mapping of its route. Simpson and Dick, however,
spent days going from ruin to ruin, measuring, marveling,
reconstructing in imagination, and assigning names by
transliterating the words of their guide: Una Vida, Hungo
Pavie, Chetro Kettle, Bonito, Penasca Blanca. *(Figs. 23 and
25)* They sat among the debris, like Gibbon at sunset in the
church of the Zoccolanti or Henry Adams on the steps of
Santa Maria di Ara Coeli, imagining the original and trying
to deduce the origins, decline, and fall. They knew their
Prescott and thought these walls must have been laid by

11. Gregg, *Commerce of the Prairies*, p. 197.

twelfth-century Aztecs or perhaps the earlier Toltecs. Dick, elaborating an idea which he had read in Josiah Gregg, suggested their original design—three or four terraced stories facing a court, with unbroken walls rising the whole height on the outer face. He sketched a reconstructed version of Hungo Pavie, missing the correct number of levels by one (as Simpson pointed out in his report) and envisioning far too precise and angular a structure, but beautifully illustrating his correct concept of the terraces.

Their work in Chaco Canyon was highly significant. They described and mapped all of the principal ruins, overlooking only Pueblo Alto, and the names they first recorded, even the word Chaco itself, have all been retained, though occasionally modified in spelling. Their descriptions formed the basis of all the succeeding accounts for the next thirty years. It is true that Dick's ground plans, compared with those of twentieth-century archaeologists, tend to be too regular, the angles too exact, the rooms too uniform; but he was working against time in rubble which he could not clear away. Even so, particularly with Hungo Pavie and Wijiji, the Kern plans are remarkably similar to later reconstructions.[12]

Preoccupied as they were with their scientific adventures, the Kerns yet noted the waning of the expedition's success as far as Navajo relations were concerned. On August 31 Dick matter-of-factly described in his journal what may

12. Donald D. Brand, F. M. Hawley, et al., *Tseh So* (Albuquerque, 1937), p. 20; Cosmos Mindeleff, *The Cliff Ruins of Canyon de Chelly* (Washington, 1897), p. 80. Anthropologists find important clues to climatic changes in the Simpson–Kern record of the Chaco River in August flowing eight feet wide and one and a half feet deep, a stream which a hundred years later is completely dry; Simpson, *Navajo Journal*, p. 37; Edgar L. Hewett, *Chaco Canyon* (Albuquerque, 1936), pp. 16, 125. For a comparison with modern workers take Simpson, *Navajo Journal*, Pls. 27, 30, 33, and 37 to compare with Harold Gladwin, *Chaco Branch* (Globe, Ariz.), p. 102; Florence Hawley, *Significance of the Dated Prehistory of Chetro Ketl* (Albuquerque, 1934), Pl. 10; and George Pepper, *Pueblo Bonito* (New York, 1920), fig. 155.

well be one of the decisive events in the history of Navajo
and white contact:

> Navajoes crowding around us in great numbers. Coun-
> cil met. Agreed to the terms and some agreed to meet us
> at Che in person and the two old chiefs Narbona (head
> chief) and Jose Largo by deputy. . . . The council was
> dissolved, when a Spaniard [one of the Mexican volun-
> teers] said a horse had been stolen from him some time
> ago. The horse was among the Navajoes and he could
> identify him. The Col. ordered the horse to be given
> up. The Mexican advanced to get him, when Narbona
> said something in Navajo and the horseman rode off.
> Col. W. gave the word to fire. The guard did so & at
> the first shot the Indians broke and fled up a ravine to
> the N[orth]. The six pounder was fired 3 times at them,
> and a force sent in pursuit. Narbona the head chief was
> shot in 4 or 5 places and scalped.

Up to that time the expedition might reasonably have
hoped for some positive results with the Navajo. But after
the death of Narbona, only failure rode at its side.

Narbona, whom Dick once described as a "wise and great
warrior," was a giant of a man both physically and politi-
cally: six and a half feet tall and as close to being the head
chieftain as the Navajo political structure allowed. He was
reputed to be ninety years old and in Navajo councils had
long and genuinely sought peace with the white men. His
murder by the whites over the claim of one Mexican for a
horse, at a time when thousands of horses were being stolen
by both Mexican and Indian, turned the expedition into
a mockery. In the excitement Ned and Dick did not think
to preserve Narbona's skull for Morton. They were later
furious with themselves for the oversight, and Dick wrote,
"I think he had the finest head I ever saw on an Indian."[13]

13. Both Dick's "warrior" and "head" quotes are from R. Kern to Samuel
Morton, July 3, 1850, Newberry Library.

The day after Narbona's murder they pushed through a
narrow, dangerous defile and emerged among fir and white
oak on an elevated plain below which lay the escarped fissure of Chelly. It was the heart of Navajoland; Simpson
called it the "ultima thule" of the expedition. The Kerns
watched as the Army crushed Indian cornfields, and they
thought of the silent Navajos whom they knew stood concealed, watching, behind every rock. When Talking God
had given corn to White-shell Woman, he had said, "There
is no better thing than this in the world, for it is the gift
of life."

> Since the ancient days, I have planted,
> Since the time of emergence, I have planted,
> The great corn-plant I have planted, . . .
>
> Truly in the East
> The white bean
> And the great corn-plant
> Are tied with the white lightning.

As the troops circled to the north of the hugh three-
pronged chasm, heading toward the Navajo villages at its
western mouth, the Kerns had a preliminary peep over the
edge of the precipice, some eight hundred feet deep at that
point. "The stream winding through seemed like a small
thread." Somewhere in this vast fissure lay a legendary
secret fortress fifteen ladders high—a Navajo retreat in time
of danger which no white man had yet entered. As the Army
approached, the Kerns watched "the huts of the enemy, one
after another, springing up into smoke and flame, and their
owners scampering off in flight," to the safety of the fifteen
ladders.[14]

Early on the morning of September 8, the Kerns accompanied Simpson, a few officers, and an escort of sixty men

14. The "stream" quote is from R. Kern, Journal, Sept. 5, 1849; the
burning huts, from Simpson, *Navajo Journal*, p. 70.

on a reconnaissance of the canyon. They entered the deep trough at its mouth, expecting to find the fabled fort within a few miles. The narrow alluvial bottom, still shaded by the perpendicular walls, was colored here and there with corn-fields, melon patches, and the soft green of peach orchards. The few Navajos who had not fled occasionally appeared from their hogans to pacify the invader with baskets or blankets full of ripe peaches. Others, more fearful or hostile, watched from the cliffs above, horses and riders small and black against the sky.

Pursuing mile after mile of lateral canyons and doubling back to take other branches, they found abandoned storied pueblos, similar to the Chaco sites, but no fifteen-ladder fort. They saw the clay-plastered walls of Casa Blanca, tucked in a high niche, and sketched them "with the stupendous rocks in rear and overhanging them."[15] (Figs. 26–28) Casa Blanca seemed to them pale in comparison with a legendary fortress, as the Zuñi pueblos had appeared color-less to Coronado when his brain whirled with Cibola. After a penetration of some nine miles, they turned back. Simpson wrote that the myth of the canyon's fort was exploded.

The Navajos apparently decided that an attack on 350 armed men would be unwise. The day following the pene-tration of their canyon they signed a treaty with the United States, an act of pure expediency. The white man, talking peace, had violated their country, murdered and scalped Narbona, cut fields of corn, and by entering had desecrated their sacred canyon. The easiest way to get him out would

15. Simpson, *Navajo Journal*, p. 75; cf. the R. Kern drawing lithographed opposite p. 74. According to Dr. David DeHarport of Harvard University's Peabody Museum, the party went first up Cottonwood Canyon, retraced its steps and then proceeded up the main artery to Wild Cherry Canyon, some-times called Spring. This was less than one-fourth of the total length of the canyon. Even on their route they missed several important archaeological sites, but DeHarport feels that the real significance of this expedition was in awakening the public to the ancient monuments of the Southwest.

be to sign his meaningless treaty.[16] To expedite matters, they cleverly spread a rumor that the Apaches were attacking Zuñi, where Indians friendly to the whites might desperately need help.

From the Navajo standpoint the rumor worked, and the day after the treaty Colonel Washington hustled his troops toward the south. The Kerns were not overly concerned by the detour. They found the afternoons "soft, balmy and autumnal." They lightheartedly sketched the sandstone formations along the route and labeled them: Punch mug, olive jar, "William Penn with his broad brimmed beaver and inflated by a hearty meal."[17] There were always birds to catch and snakes to trap.

At Zuñi no one knew anything of an Apache raid, though there had been trouble with Navajos. The Army stayed, therefore, less than a day, but that was long enough for the Kerns to record more local legends. Here they compensated too for their failure to collect Narbona's head. They heard that the body of a Navajo killed in the recent raid still lay in a field nearby. Dick rode out, like Perseus, brought back the head and later sent it triumphantly to Morton.[18]

Before the expedition ended, they added one more archaeological adventure. Hearing that a bit south of the Army's route between Zuñi and Laguna was a jutting bluff, called Morro, covered with half an acre of inscriptions, Dick and Simpson were intrigued. Most of the other men laughed at the stories; "all gammon," they said, and Simpson, too, was somewhat skeptical. Dick was, however, the man of curiosity—as Simpson said, "ever zealous in an enterprise of this kind." Ned unfortunately had to stay, again, with the Army, to fulfill his obligations in mapping the route. Dick and Simpson rode all morning through fantastic for-

16. Twelve men, including Richard Kern, witnessed the document; James Calhoun, *Official Correspondence* (Washington, 1915), p. 25.

17. Both quotes are from R. Kern, Journal, 1849.

18. R. Kern to S. Morton, July 3, 1850. Simpson's version differs: *Navajo Journal*, p. 94.

mations—steamboats and Egyptian tombs—and when they reached Morro Rock, they found on walls as smooth as clay a long series of Spanish inscriptions—names of explorers, governors, traders—interspersed with Indian hieroglyphics. At least ten were dated in the seventeenth century, the earliest 1606. Simpson and Dick started immediately making facsimiles and worked from noon to sunset without finishing. Simpson was so excited that he could not sleep that night. The next morning the two were up at three in order to start by dawn light. When they had copied every word, Dick chiseled a few more: "Lt. J. H. Simpson, U.S.A., and R. H. Kern, artist, visited and copied these inscriptions, September 17, 1849."

Back with the troops, they traveled through Laguna and Albuquerque and closed the circle at Santa Fe. "All that could be accomplished by the expedition, then, may be considered as having been accomplished," wrote Simpson. As far as pacifying the Navajos, nothing could be further from the truth. But for the Kerns, for two developing frontier artists and scientific explorers, the expedition had real meaning. Simpson had been a valuable companion, a scientist with as great a backlog of topographical experience as Frémont's; and there seems to have grown between Simpson and the Kerns a much warmer comradeship than Frémont ever allowed.

Although Ned had observed native peoples in California, it was this Navajo expedition which really sharpened him as an ethnologist. As a member of the Philadelphia Academy his scientific interests were much wider than on his earlier ventures. As far as we know, for example, Ned never collected an Indian skull in California! And he had gained on this Navajo trip important additional experience in topography. Ned's map appeared in the Simpson journal and was incorporated in the Parke–Kern map of 1851, which in turn became the basis of southwestern geographical knowledge for the next ten years.

From this expedition the Kerns, especially Dick, devel-

oped an increasing interest in the early history of the Southwest. Among the available printed sources they found Josiah Gregg the most reliable, while Ruxton and Emory and
Abert were dismissed as at best historically inaccurate.[19]
The pueblo ruins aroused their deepest curiosity, and they
mused, as have so many since, over the contrast between the
high level of culture represented in the Chaco and the lesser
accomplishments of the contemporary Pueblo Indians. Dick
wrote to Spruce M. Baird, an archaeologically minded Indian agent at Albuquerque who would become a good
friend, and Baird sent back some reading matter as well as
advice for future visits—examine for the marks of edged
tools, aqueducts, and remains of domestic vegetation.[20] In
Dick the ruins excited a wonder about the sixteenth-century Spanish search for Cibola, and he and Simpson began
to speculate about the actual route of Coronado's march
and the location of the Seven Cities. When he found time
in ensuing months, Dick rummaged through documents in
the governor's palace and perfected his Spanish to read
them. Even after Dick left Santa Fe, his friends there were
still copying sixteenth-century manuscripts for him.

The Navajo expedition confirmed the Kerns' desire to
stay awhile in New Mexico. They could have gotten home
easily enough now. They had a little money, but through
contacts with the Army they could have traveled with government supply trains to Fort Leavenworth. Too, their
concern over Ben's body had perforce become but a black
shadow in the backs of their minds: on the Navajo expedition they had used the contacts with distant Indians to seek
further information about Ben's murder, and at one point
in their questioning they even met a Hopi (they used the
term Moqui) who knew Old Bill Williams. But by the summer of 1850 Ned's thoughts must have been much like

19. R. Kern to S. Morton, July 3, 1850.
20. S. Baird to R. Kern, March 30, 1851, Fort Sutter Papers.

Dick's: "I do not think I shall ever allude again in public
to our disaster in the San Juan Mountains . . . the subject
is a very painful one to me, and I speak of it as little as
possible. I am willing to leave it with the past."[21]

New Mexico at the moment seemed an interesting part
of the world, exciting and unusual. And the demand for
their skills ran high. There was little break in their work.
The assembling and ordering of the data from the Navajo
expedition had still to be done, and for any such project
the subsequent desk activity was as important as the field
notes. In Santa Fe, Ned analyzed journals, plotted astronomical observations, and produced the map which appeared in Simpson's official report. Dick redrew his sketches,
as well as a few of Ned's, for the lithographer. Simpson kept
the Kerns on his payroll until the day after Christmas, 1849,
when work on the Navajo expedition was finally completed.[22]

During 1850 one job led to another. The Army, finally
realizing the ineffectiveness of its present garrisons, was
engaged in moving men and equipment from the towns to
more strategic posts at the approaches to the settled areas,
and topographers were needed to ascertain the best sites—
men with not only a knowledge of the passes and trails but
also with skills in locating dependable supplies of water,
wood, and forage grass.

The Kerns were hired on occasion by each successive
commanding officer of the Topographical Corps, giving a
continuity in the field which the Army itself did not provide. Late in 1849 with Simpson they reconnoitered the
country around Cebolleta (along a tributary of the San
Jose River) to find the proper location for a fort thus deep

21. For the Hopi who knew Williams see R. Kern, Journal, 1849. The
quote is from R. Kern to S. Morton, July 3, 1850. The matter did come
up again, however: J. Greiner to R. Kern, Jan. 27, 1852, Fort Sutter Papers.

22. J. Simpson to J. Abert, April 13, 1850, Old Army Branch, National
Archives.

in Navajo country. The Kerns probably also helped Simpson in a survey of the Ocate and Rayado rivers and of the route from Santa Fe to Donaña and El Paso. When Simpson, whose general unhappiness with New Mexico was intensified by a tooth ailment and erysipelas, was recalled, his successor, Lt. John Parke, hired Dick to help incorporate all the recent explorations into an extensive map of the territory. When Lt. John Pope supplanted Parke in the summer of 1851, one of Pope's first dispatches to his commanding officer in Washington commented on his good fortune in having the Kerns still available.[23]

Nor were their talents in demand only with the Topographical Corps. While Simpson was still in New Mexico in March of 1850, Captain Henry Judd of the artillery took Dick on a reconnaissance from Las Vegas along the fertile bottom lands of the Pecos River to the Bosque Grande (near the later Fort Sumner). Dick worked on the Pecos map until July. Later he did some charting and computing for the Census Marshal.[24]

The fall and winter of 1850–51 were relatively quiet for topographical work in New Mexico, and during this time both of the Kerns were forced into jobs less appropriate to their skills. On July 1, 1850, Ned became a forage master for the Quartermaster Corps with a salary of forty dollars a month. This involved a move to the little village of Abiquiu on the old Spanish Trail about fifty miles northwest of Santa Fe, but it is possible that Ned appreciated the move, and he may even have sought it. His health was not

23. The suppositions that the Kerns accompanied Simpson on the 1850 expeditions are purely circumstantial; but see Simpson, *Navajo Journal*, Appendix; J. Simpson to J. Abert, March 22, 1850, Old Army Branch, National Archives; R. Kern to S. Morton, July 3, 1850. For the Parke–Kern map of 1851 see Carl Wheat, *Mapping the Transmississippi West* (San Francisco, 1959), *3*, 19–22. For reference to Pope's comment on Kern see J. Abert to J. Pope, Sept. 25, 1851, Old Army Branch, National Archives.

24. C. Hoppin to J. R. Bartlett, Jan. 23, 1851, Bartlett Papers, John Carter Brown Library.

good at the time; perhaps his epilepsy created the need for seclusion.

Later that summer and all through the next winter and spring, Dick also worked for the quartermaster as clerk and storekeeper in the clothing depot at Santa Fe.[25] He received ten dollars a month more than his brother but apparently did not have to work terribly hard. At the same time he was clothing clerk he was doing so much topography and sketching for Parke that he had to turn down an offer from John Bartlett to help with the Mexican Boundary Surveys.

The Kerns never ceased collecting. Large agglomerations of pressed plants and preserved bugs they crated and sent to the Academy of Natural Sciences, and their room in Santa Fe was cluttered with stuffed birds, the beginnings of another collection like the one they had lost in the mountains.[26]

Long before Ned left for Abiquiu, the brothers had set up a cooperative mess, sharing costs with a few bachelor friends. Their circle of acquaintances had widened. They were active Oddfellows, as they had been in Philadelphia, and the Santa Fe lodge throve as vigorously as their home chapter. Among the fraternal brothers was one of their closest Santa Fe friends, young Horace L. Dickinson, and the lodge also brought them close to such local bigwigs as Charles Blumner, treasurer of the territory. There were frequent sprees; as Dickinson said, "Having a *bust* is . . . quite proper to a resident of Santa Fe or Taos." The Christmas of 1850 occasioned a binge which they were still writing about a year later.[27]

The circle undoubtedly missed Ned when he went to

25. Capt. L. C. Easton, Reports on Persons Employed at Santa Fe, 1850–51, Old Army Branch, National Archives.

26. R. Kern to J. R. Bartlett, March 14, 1851; Bartlett Papers, John Carter Brown Library; variant copy in Fort Sutter Papers.

27. H. Dickinson to E. Kern, Sept. 10, 1851, and Jan. 27, 1852, Fort Sutter Papers.

Abiquiu, and perhaps that is why the following spring they saw to it that he was nominated to a job in Santa Fe, that of engrossing-and-enrolling clerk for the House of Representatives of the territorial legislature. On the first day of the first session, Spruce Baird placed Ned's name in nomination and he was unanimously elected. Perhaps health had improved; in any case, he returned, and for some forty days he engrossed the bills of the first session and received one hundred and twenty-nine dollars.[28]

Such diversions from the Kerns' professional work bespoke the end of their usefulness in New Mexico. By the summer of 1851 both Ned and Dick were back with topography, but each of their new surveying jobs took them out of New Mexico on a long route toward home. They left the territory as if thrown by centrifugal force, each flying out at the same time but in opposite directions. Dick went westward with Lt. Lorenzo Sitgreaves and Lt. John Parke to survey the Zuñi River to its supposed junction with the Colorado. Ned headed north and east, blazing an improved route between New Mexico and Fort Leavenworth. In early August, 1851, Ned and Dick said goodbye to one another and to Santa Fe, hoping perhaps for Christmas together in Philadelphia.

Ned's expedition was intended to forge a better link with the states, especially for the sake of the new Fort Union, where the Santa Fe troops had moved under the Army's revised policy of stations outside of the towns. The fort, east of the Sangre de Cristos where the Bent's Fort and Cimarron trails converged, needed improved communications, and Captain John Pope, the brash successor to Parke as chief topographical officer in the department, was ordered to find a more direct and easier route to Missouri. To help, Pope hired Ned.

28. New Mexico Territorial Legislature, *Journal of the House of Representatives*, 1st Session, June–July, 1851. Misc. Treasury Acct. 117404, First Auditor's Office, No. 62 and 80, Fiscal Branch, National Archives.

The expedition gathered at Barclay's Fort, a few sprawling adobe walls along the Mora River a short distance from Fort Union. *(Fig. 38)* Ned wrote cryptically that "The Male and Female brought me safe to Barcley's Fort . . . according to contract," and not long after, "we left the beaten track for the Lord only knew where . . . ."[29]

Ned was right. The old "track" was indeed beaten. The Cimarron route had a way of crossing innumerable streams (Cottonwood Creek, McNees Creek, Sand Creek, and a dozen others) at right angles rather than following them for any distance. Since much of the country was arid, these crossings inevitably became campsites. And with the immense increase in Santa Fe traffic following the Mexican War (Simpson alone in the fall of 1850 passed more than three hundred wagons between Big Timbers and Leavenworth), the sites were denuded of wood and grass with water supplies reduced to muddy, stinking pools. Pope and Kern hoped to find a trail which would follow stream courses and thus to eliminate the necessity of repeated camping in the same spots; avoid sandy stretches and mountain passes, like the Raton on the Bent's Fort route; and, if possible, shorten the distance.

They followed the regular Cimarron Trail by Wagon Mound and Rabbit Ear Creek to Cedar Springs (from northeastern New Mexico to southeastern Colorado). It was there they left the "beaten track," crossing over a divide to Two Butte Creek, running its whole length to the Arkansas River at Chouteau's Island (not far from the present Kansas–Colorado border). Thus far Pope felt they had been "successful beyond my most sanguine expectations."[30] They

29. This and all subsequent Kern quotations on the Pope Expedition, unless otherwise identified, are from E. Kern, Journal, 1851, Huntington Library.

30. J. Pope to J. Abert, Sept. 18, 1851, Old Army Branch, National Archives.

had found abundant wood and grass and water, and the Indians had even been friendly enough to offer Ned a "muchacha." Pope sent an express rider to Fort Union with news of the route and expected the government supply train to break the new road within the month.

From the Arkansas on, they were not so fortunate. Turning north to the Smoky Hill Fork of the Kansas, they found the country, in Ned's words, "so much broken as to render it almost impracticable for wagons."[31] Furthermore, among the rattlesnake nests along the Smoky Hill, the Arapahos stampeded nearly half of their animals. Leaving a cache under a bluish-yellow cliff, Pope and Ned with three others pushed ahead for help. Their animals ("broken down Drg [dragoon] horses & mules mixed") in turn gave out miles before they reached Council Grove, and then, as Ned wrote, "we took it afoot." It would have been unlike Ned's fate had circumstances been otherwise. None of his western expeditions was without a period of desperation and this, his last, was no exception.

Though Fort Leavenworth ended their reconnaissance, Ned went on to St. Louis with Pope to help prepare the map. While working over field notes, they came to a disturbing conclusion. On the trail they had noticed discrepancies between their observations and those made earlier by Frémont. Ned had written in his diary that Frémont's position for Sand Creek "must be in error, a great mistake." Now they confirmed what they had suspected, that the Pathfinder's 1845 map was in places grossly inaccurate. Their examination of the Smoky Hill Fork, according to Pope, "exhibited nothing resembling the sketch of Capt. Frémont . . . his position for Bent's Fort is *40* miles too far west," Big Sand Creek was sixteen miles off, and "the big bend of the Smoky Hill Fork is really a degree too far to the

31. E. Kern to [Simpson?], Oct., 1851, Fort Sutter Papers.

East." He called the earlier map erroneous, inaccurate, and useless.[32] Thus to Ned's case against Frémont was now added a substantial charge of incompetence.

Two weeks after the report was finished Ned was home, sleeping at 62 Filbert Street after almost exactly two years.[33] He had left this house for California with a poetic glow, his two favorite brothers with him, confident in his commander. He returned alone, saddened, with bitterness, and eyes that darkened at the mention of Frémont. But these two years had seen Ned achieve his own stature, emerge from the shadow of Frémont to assume in his own right the position of a qualified topographer, western artist, and scientist. Catlin once said that the wilderness was "the true school of the arts."[34] In Ned's case, it seems to have been true. Though his best work was still ahead of him, his years of practice in the West had much improved his competence in sketching, and his surveying and scientific skills would make him valuable to expeditions anywhere in the world.

Money was a problem, and he tried to profit from land bounties granted to veterans. Late in 1851 he filed his first claim for eighty acres, based on his services at Fort Sutter. But his agent in Washington could promise no speedy action, for, as he said, "There always has been and still is

32. J. Pope to J. Abert, Sept. 18, 1851. The Department rapped Pope's knuckles for this comment on Frémont; J. Abert to J. Pope, Oct. 27, 1851, Old Army Branch, National Archives. Frémont himself never claimed absolute accuracy. On the third expedition he found errors in his own previous map amounting in one instance to 15′ in longitude; G. K. Warren, "Epitome," in George M. Wheeler, *Report upon United States Geographical Surveys* . . . (Washington, 1889), p. 558.

33. Ned took Pope's report (in which Pope included high commendation for Kern) east with him to deliver in Washington, but he was taken ill in Philadelphia, hence sent the report on from there; E. Kern to J. Abert, Oct. 1, 1851; Old Army Branch, National Archives.

34. George Catlin, *Letters and Notes on . . . the North American Indians* (2 vols. London, 1841), *1*, 15.

much difficulty in regard to everything relating to Fremonts doings in California."[35]

Through November and December there was no word from Dick. This would perhaps have bothered Ned less if the shadow of Ben's murder did not still lay heavy on him and his older brothers and sisters. But they could reason away fears with the thought that Dick was irrepressible; it would take a pretty tough Indian to get him—an Indian at least as tough at the Utes who got Ben, and certainly not the skulking, miserable creatures of the Great Basin. Ned knew the weakness and cowardice of these tribes well enough, or he knew rather their Humboldt River counterparts, and he assured the family that one of Dick's mighty laughs or even one of his noisy puns would send them scampering, might even impale them on the nearest "Jeremiah" tree.

Early the next year word came. It was a long letter from Ned's California friend, George McKinstry, now in San Diego where he had stumbled across Dick. He snickered at Dick's "agreeable trip over the desert. . . . He came in fat and saucy having been well fed on mule beef and roasted Jack Ass."[36] Ned guessed that Dick had had a rough time of it.

Not long after, Dick himself arrived from San Francisco by way of Panama. The homecoming was joyous, marred only by the absence of Ben. Ned had been the center of attention in 1847, but now it was Dick, since he was the last to arrive. And Ned was the one now hungry for every detail.

After their parting in Santa Fe, Dick had moved out to Zuñi where he and Parke were to join the Sitgreaves expe-

35. R. Burgess to E. Kern, Nov. 4, 1851, Fort Sutter Papers. It was not until April 1853 that the warrant was issued and not until 1858 that he was able to sell it. In 1856 Edward filed a claim for a second eighty acres under the Act of 1855. Claims of Nov. 12, 1851, and Jan. 31, 1856, and warrant of April 19, 1853, all in Interior Branch, National Archives.

36. G. McKinstry to E. Kern, Dec. 23, 1851, Fort Sutter Papers.

dition on a route which was almost unknown as far as the Army was concerned. Instructions even implied that the Zuñi River, which they were to explore, flowed either directly into the main Colorado or into the Gila; but neither conjecture was true and both overlooked the existence of the Little Colorado. The Army knew well the Gila route to the south, and Frémont had mapped the trails to the north, but this area in between still bore the scrawl "Unexplored" on the maps of 1851.

From the Zuñi cornfields the expedition followed a trail to the Little Colorado River, along which they descended through sage and creosote to the falls (beyond the present town of Leupp). There they turned due west to avoid the rumored difficulties of the great gorge of the main Colorado. They must have wondered about the advantage of the turn, for the road they took became rough, cracked into "numerous deep & rugged canons, that run into one another," as Dick said, "like ones fingers."[37] The box chronometer, though packed in wool and carried by the steadiest mule, stopped from the joggling. The nights were freezing, the days hot enough to melt the bacon. Water was so scarce that they were lucky when they could spoon up a few mouthfuls from seepage holes. Dick examined the Wupatki ruins (finding ancient pueblos was by now commonplace), and explained their abandonment as having been due to lack of water. The comment had a highly personal significance. Supplies ran low, and diarrhea resulted from their diet of mule meat. The Yampai Indians were a constant nuisance and an occasional menace—one arrow penetrated Dick's bedroll, but he fortunately was not in it at the time. Irritation and hatred of the Indians rose until at one point the expedition deliberately planted a pile of mule meat and biscuit "with plenty of arsenic in them in hopes some of the Indians may get them."

37. This and all subsequent quotations from Kern on Sitgreaves Expedition are from R. Kern, Journal, 1851, Huntington Library.

Dick was, of course, recreating a kind of period familiar to the Kerns, one of gloom. He described nights when he couldn't sleep, when strange "feelings of old times" came over him.

But he told of loveliness as well: autumn aspen groves on the San Francisco Mountains ("thick white trunks and yellowish leaves gave one an idea of a newly whitewashed room, so bright every thing seemed"); scarlet ocotilla blossoms, which he called St. Joseph's Rod; the sunlight falling on "a rich compound of bright yellow, sienna, green, carmine & gray"; and, before the dry jornadas, the clear headwaters of Bill Williams River. Here Dick could report to Ned a piece of satisfying news. Their guide had said he had met Old Bill Williams as early as 1837 where this stream met the Colorado, so Dick, taking advantage of his mapping position, named the stream on his sketches the Bill Williams Fork, thereby making of the river a memorial to their friend.[38]

For twenty-five days they straggled 243 miles down the big Colorado River to the Gila, stayed at Fort Yuma long enough to conclude technically the expedition, then proceeded across desert and coast range to San Diego. Here around the officers' barracks Dick met McKinstry. It was a wild place with each of the high-strung officers acting like a "loose bull," as McKinstry put it. Dick went north to San Francisco, probably to get quicker transportation home, and McKinstry gave him a letter of introduction to John Sutter. Dick was warmly entertained by the old man, who reminisced at length about Ned and the days of '46. "I hope yet that your brother will come here," he sighed, "in a land where 1000 of chances are for one in comparison with an old country."

---

38. Cf. interpretation in Favour, *Old Bill Williams*, p. 181, with those in Lorenzo Sitgreaves, *Report of an Expedition* (Washington, 1853), p. 13, and R. Kern, Journal, 1851, entry Oct. 23.

Dick conveyed Sutter's best regards in the form of a photograph sent especially to Ned.[39]

For Dick the Sitgreaves Expedition had meant two things: an intensification of his interest in southwestern history and a much clearer conception of the proper route for the transcontinental railroad. For Henry Schoolcraft's study of the American Indians he composed a scholarly essay and map, tracing Coronado's explorations.[40] His concern over the Pacific railroad catapulted him into an even more spectacular position, and he became a much quoted authority in the national debate over the choice of routes. Ned, who never became quite so excited over the subject, joked that his brother was becoming a "sort of Chief of Roads."[41]

Their position in the art world had also been enhanced by their experiences. In 1852, for example, Dick wrote from Washington to Ned in Philadelphia, "There is a devil-

39. The "loose bull" quote is from G. McKinstry to E. Kern, Dec. 23, 1851, Fort Sutter Papers. J. Sutter to R. Kern, Jan. 10, 1852, Huntington Library.

40. Schoolcraft, *Indian Tribes, 4,* 32–39; R. Kern to H. Schoolcraft, April 20, 1853, Schoolcraft Papers, Library of Congress. Simpson later used this article as a principal reference in "Coronado's March," *Annual Report of the Smithsonian Institution, 1869* (Washington, 1871).

41. E. Kern, Journal, 1851, back leaves. The United States Senate heard Dick's knowledge of the trans-Mississippi west described as "unequaled"; *Cong. Globe,* 32nd Cong., 2nd Sess., pp. 422–23. For Senator William M. Gwin of California he wrote a twenty-four page essay favoring the route which later became, roughly speaking, the Santa Fe Railroad, and on January 17, 1853, Gwin read the entire document to the Senate. Dick's aches and thirsts with Sitgreaves echoed when he described "the uninhabitable deserts" between the Little Colorado and the Sierra Nevada, but he compared an account of the Humboldt route which Ned drew up for him, added snow and lack of population, saw too little timber on the El Paso–Gila route, and decided that the "uninhabitable deserts" of his way were less formidable than the obstacles on any other. R. Kern to W. Gwin, Jan. 10, 1853, Fort Sutter Papers; *Cong. Globe,* 32nd Cong., 2nd Sess., pp. 320–21. When Gwin, who agreed with Dick, finally pushed through an appropriation for surveying the routes, the Santa Fe *Gazette* (March 26, 1853) editorialized that for this service New Mexico owed "none more than our friend R. H. Kern, who was for some years a resident of our territory; he has done us a noble act of kindness for which we trust our citizens will in some appropriate manner express their thanks."

ish little miniature painter from Boston, Stagg [Richard M. Staigg], a good painter; we are great chums. He looks at me with veneration because I've seen such places."[42] About the same time, they were friendly with David Houghton, the portraitist, and Jasper Cropsey, then a member of the National Academy, as Staigg was to be later. They undoubtedly knew John Chapman, probably James Hamilton, and about this time Ned very likely met John Mix Stanley, if he had not known him earlier. He and Stanley were both frequenting Washington, had similar interests, and Ned owned one of Stanley's oils, "Portrait of An Artist."[43]

The two restless Kern brothers were looking for a job. It was a time when the nation was extending expansive feelers in many directions, some far beyond the continent. Surveys were planned in Central America, South America, and the Far Pacific, usually geared to commercial expansion and conducted by the Navy. Ned's first offer came from his friend Simpson, who wanted Ned to join him for topographical work in Minnesota, but through a fault in communications, this job did not materialize. He did, however, estimate equipment for western expeditions and, like Dick, wrote about Indians for Henry Schoolcraft.[44] But he began to see that the opportunities for topographical work were widen-

42. R. Kern to E. Kern, May 2, 1852, Huntington Library.

43. The Philadelphia Academy of Fine Arts, *Catalogue of the 35th Annual Exhibition* (Philadelphia, 1858). One wonders who was the subject of the painting. John Stanley, as a matter of fact, was much like Edward Kern. Both worked west in the 1840's; both spent similar periods in Santa Fe and California; both served the Topographical Corps; both assisted the Pacific Railroad Surveys, though Ned only indirectly through his brother; and both early practiced with the daguerreotype, each preparing an apparatus in the spring of 1853. As draughtsmen they both varied considerably from work to work. At their worst (as in Edward's drawings of the California Indians *(Fig. 11)* or Stanley's "Prairie Indian Encampment") they drew the human figure clumsily. But at other times (in Kern's rendering of Chukchis playing games *(Fig. 50)* or Stanley's "Buffalo Hunt on the Southwestern Prairies") they imbued bodies with fresh buoyant action.

44. J. Simpson to R. Kern, May 11, 1852, Huntington Library. Fragment, n.d., MS 147, Fort Sutter Papers. Schoolcraft, *Indian Tribes*, 5, 649–50.

ing. He became particularly intrigued with news accounts concerning Matthew Calbraith Perry's expedition to the shores of Japan. Friends in Washington assured him that for such a venture the Navy should need artist–topographers, so a month after Perry's appointment Ned applied to the Commodore for a position. Perry referred the application to the Secretary of the Navy, who answered that the Department did not intend to make such an appointment.[45]

Shortly thereafter Ned did, however, find a berth to Japan with the North Pacific Expedition of Commander Cadwalader Ringgold at a salary of eight hundred dollars a year plus the rations and rating of a Master's Mate.[46] Ned knew little of the sea, only what a passenger coming once around the Horn would remember, but he had known little of the plains when he left Westport in 1845. True, in 1853 it would have seemed more logical that he go West again, to work with Simpson in Minnesota or to assist with the Pacific Railroad surveys. But to Ned a Japanese pagoda suddenly seemed more exciting than a New Mexican adobe. Some of his friends in the Santa Fe *Weekly Gazette* called it a Quixotic fancy that the government should explore foreign countries with so much remaining to do at home. It would be far better, they said, to "open" New Mexico with better roads and mails than to worry about Japan, five thousand miles away. But Ned could justly say he had done his share in opening New Mexico, and he could rationalize that Dick, "the Chief of Roads," was still carrying on, even if he was not.

Dick, meanwhile, was hired for the surveys which in 1853 were initiated over most of the West in hopes of determin-

45. E. Kern to W. A. Graham, May 24, 1852; W. A. Graham to E. Kern, May 31, 1852, Navy Branch, National Archives. The Department did appoint William Heine as artist and Eliphalet Brown as daguerreotypist for the expedition. Dick had earlier put out feelers for the position, but had decided against it. W. Jeffers to R. Kern, April 28, 1852, Huntington Library.

46. C. Ringgold to J. Kennedy, March 2, 1853, Navy Branch, National Archives.

ing the single most feasible route for the transcontinental
railroad. He had had other offers, such as one from E. G.
Squier to help on Nicaraguan railroad surveys, but his concern over the Pacific railroad kept him closer home.[47]
He was to sketch and map the 38th parallel under Captain
John W. Gunnison of the Topographical Corps, a handsome, forty-year-old West Pointer with much of the right-
eousness of Simpson.

So in the spring of 1853 they parted again, Ned on a
highly exotic venture; Dick on what had become for the
Kerns a more routine assignment. Much of the 38th parallel
was all too familiar, and included on the trip was Frederick
Creutzfeldt, the botanist whom Dick had known with Frémont in 1848; the two could now reminisce once more at
Westport in June, while they packed the boxes of sextants,
theodolites, and barometers.

Again the mules were wild on the first catching up. (Gunnison moaned, "such a muss as fifty Jackasses of brutes and
a dozen of asses of men can make . . .")[48] Again torrential
rains. ("All is *green,* the ground, the men & the business.")
Again the careful comparison of maps, now including the
one which Ned and Pope had drawn twenty-one months
before. Again the Arkansas and the Spanish Peaks, this time
seen in summer rather than in snow. Again over the Sangre
de Cristos into the upper Rio Grande Valley, where they
might conceivably stumble over Ben's bones. Across the San
Juan Mountains, now dark with the green of August, so
unlike the cold glare of 1848. Through Cochetopa Pass, an
easy trail mocking the nearby sharp, tangled ridges which

47. R. Kern to E. G. Squier, Jan. 1, 1853, Squier Papers, Library of Congress. Dick preferred to go on his chosen Albuquerque route, but Benton
and Secretary of War Jefferson Davis conspired against him. He wrote J. S.
Phelps, May 29, 1853 (Yale University Library) that he had been "Made like
the great Clay another martyr to the compromise—mine dwindling down
from the whole Union, to old Bullion's."

48. This and the following quote are from J. Gunnison to M. Gunnison,
June 19, 1853, Huntington Library.

Dick and Creutzfeldt had fought in 1849. Over the divide to the river later known as the Gunnison. And eventually into the broad Sevier Valley. At this point Captain Gunnison breathed relief: "the great mountains have been passed. . . ."[49]

On October 25 Gunnison took Dick, Creutzfeldt, and a few others to explore the autumn sloughs, noisy with geese and ducks, in the direction of slowly desiccating Lake Sevier. That night they camped in a thick stand of willows. Day broke, with ice on standing water. Some of the men were already clumped around breakfast fires when "a terrific yell was raised on their left, accompanied by a discharge of rifles and a shower of arrows."[50] They were from Ute Indians on a rampage against Mormons and white men in general.

Dick and Gunnison came out of their tent, quickly saw the ambush, and tried with the others to reach their horses. "Those who succeeded, escaped; while those who failed, fell." Dick, Gunnison, Creutzfeldt, and five others died, Gunnison's body punctured with fifteen arrows, Dick's with a single rifle ball in his heart. The Indians mutilated the remains and cut from Dick's finger a bloodstone ring with the initial "K."[51] Eventually the ring found its way back

49. *Pacific Railroad Reports, 2* (13 vols. Washington, 1855), Pt. 1, p. 70.
50. R. Morris to [Adjutant General], Oct. 29, 1853, Old Army Branch, National Archives.
51. A. and R. Moran to G. Moran, Oct. 29, 1853, unidentified newspaper clipping in Gunnison correspondence, Huntington Library. An eighteen-year old assistant topographer of the expedition wrote in grief that Dick "has been as a father to me," and that the night before he died he had asked that, if he did not return, his books and paints should go to his brother Ned and his money to his sister Mary. St. Louis *Evening News,* Dec. 19, 1853, as quoted in Mumey, *John Williams Gunnison,* pp. 130–31. Cf. *Pacific Railroad Reports, 2,* Pt. 1, p. 74. Mercer, one of the participants, forty years later said Kern was standing by the fire, and Gunnison washing in the river at the time of attack; Kern was killed by the first shots, Gunnison in willows later; Josiah Gibbs, "Gunnison Massacre," *Utah Historical Quarterly, 1* (1928), 67–75. Cf. Solomon Carvalho, *Incidents of Travel,* pp. 197–99.

to the family, and they may have recalled some of Dick's favorite poetic lines:

> ... If upon the troubled sea
> Thou hast thrown a gem unheeded,
> Hope not that wind or wave shall bring
> The treasure back when needed.

It is not difficult to imagine Ned's emotions on learning of Dick's death, his tears in requiem for a second brother lying in a lonely mountain valley not far from the first, his bitter reflection that the same infectious curiosity which had already killed two Kerns still drove like a daemon the third!

> Sail forth! Steer for deep waters only!
> Restless, O Soul, exploring . . .

36. Richard Kern, *Cosniña Indians*, 1851. Lithograph. Sitgreaves, *Report* (1853).

37. Richard Kern, *Yampai Indians*, 1851. Lithograph. Sitgreaves, *Report* (1853).

38. Edward Kern, *Barclay's Fort, Mora River, New Mexico.* Diary, 1851, pencil, 5″ × 7″. H
ington Library. Compare sketch of the same scene by Richard Kern in Alexander Bar
Papers, Bancroft Library.

39. John Mix Stanley, from sketch by Richard Kern, *Peaks of the Sierra Blanca,* 1853. P
Railroad Reports (1855–60), 2.

40. John M. Stanley, from sketch by Richard Kern, *Fort Massachusetts*, 1853. *Pacific Railroad Reports* (1855–60), 2.

41. Edward Kern, *Temple Interior*, ca. 1854. Water color, 7¼″ × 11¼″. Collection of Mrs. Raoul Drapeau, Chelmsford, Massa-chusetts.

42. Edward Kern, *The Scribe, Hong Kong,* 1854. Water color, 9¾″ × 7¾″. Collection of Mrs. Raoul Drapeau, Chelmsford, Massachusetts.

43. Edward Kern, *Mandarin Palace Interior*, ca. 1854. Water color, 7″ × 10¾″. Collection of Mrs. Raoul Drapeau, Chelmsford, Massachusetts.

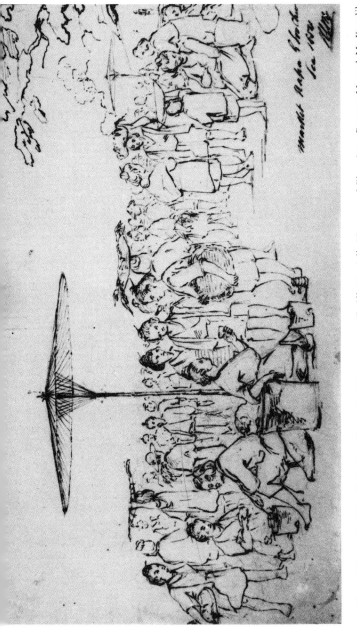

44. Edward Kern. *Market at Napa, Loo Choo.* 1854. Pen over pencil. 8″ × 13⅝″. Museum of Fine Arts. Boston. M. and M. Karolik Collection.

45. Edward Kern, *False Capstan Head*, 1854. Pen-and-ink sketch from navigational chart, *Coast of Loo Choo.* National Archives.

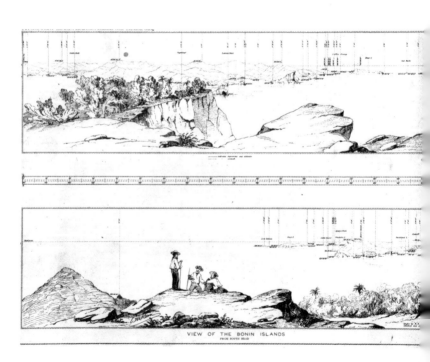

46. Edward Kern, *View of the Bonin Islands,* 1854. Cartographic pen-and-ink sketch, 16½″ × National Archives.

VIEW OF THE COAST OF JAPAN.
NORTH PACIFIC SURVEY EXPEDITION,
LT. JOHN RODGER., U.S.N. COMMANDING.
SENT TO THE NAVAL ACADEMY BY ORDER OF
ASSISTANT CHIEF, BUREAU OF NAVIGATION.

dward Kern, *View of the Coast of Japan,* 1855. Oil, 22″ × 26″. United States Naval Academy
useum.

48. Edward Kern, *Cutting Up the Whale, Glassnappe [Glazenap] Harbor*, 1855. Pencil and water color, 9⅛″ × 17⅛″. Museum of Fine Arts, Boston, M. and M. Karolik Collection.

49. Edward Kern, *Cutting Up a Whale on the West Coast of Kamchatka* (error for Glazenap Harbor), 1855, Oil, 16″ × 22″. United States Naval Academy Museum.

50. Edward Kern, *Racing Among the Tchucktches [Chukchis]*, 1855. Pencil and brown wash, 10″ × 18″. Museum of Fine Arts, Boston, M. and M. Karolik Collection.

Edward Kern, *Attack on the "Waterwitch"* (erroneous title for *Meeting Indians on the Chaco),*
ca. 1856. Pencil wash, 4¾" × 8". Gilcrease Institute, Tulsa, Oklahoma.

MEETING INDIANS ON THE CHACO.

52. [Edward Kern], *Meeting Indians on the Chaco.* Lithograph. Page, *La Plata* (1859).

53. Edward Kern, *Reconnaissance Notes from Rolla, Mo., Westward to the Gasconade*, 1861 (det
Pencil. National Archives.

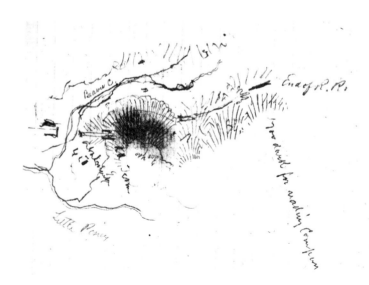

Richard Kern, *Relief Camp* [*on the Río Grande del Norte, New Mexico*], January 29, 1849. Water color, 4⅜″ × 5⅞″. Courtesy Amon Carter Museum, Fort Worth, Texas.

Smithsonian Institute
from Capitol Grounds

55. Richard Kern, *Smithsonian Institute [Institution] from Capitol Grounds.* Water color, 4⅜″ × 6″
Courtesy Amon Carter Museum, Fort Worth, Texas.

CHAPTER 5

The Vincennes

In the dawn light of June 11, 1853, the U.S.S. *Vincennes,*
sloop-of-war, flagship of a fleet of five, caught the winds
of Chesapeake Bay and sailed toward the open sea. Edward
Kern stood along the rail, watching the stiffening sails, glad
after weeks of postponed sailings, that the North Pacific
Exploring Expedition was under way. This would be Ned's
first chance to test his sea legs, and this venture, by going
eastward, the first denial of his western lodestone. Curiosity
and science know few boundaries; and an artist in a Romantic age could not help but thrill at the exotic prospects
on the other side of the world.

By noon the *Vincennes* and her four sister ships, the
John Hancock, the *John Kennedy,* the *Porpoise,* and the
Fenimore Cooper, had tacked beyond the Cape Henry
Light. Kern watched the pilot descend to his launch with
the last parcel of mail. The topsails opened full and the
salt wind scudded the sea to the eastern horizon.

Beneath Ned rolled a venerable ship, a navy veteran of
twenty-seven years. In the days of waiting he had learned

every inch of her 127-foot length and her 35-foot beam,
a fat vessel, much fatter than the clippers which so cruelly
outdistanced her (the famed clipper *Flying Cloud,* for example, was over a hundred feet longer, but only seven feet
broader), but withal a ship of proportion and dignity, well
adapted to the scientific pursuits on which she embarked.[1]

They headed across the Atlantic to round the Cape and
traverse the Indian Ocean into the western Pacific. Ned
had not seen Pacific waters since he had left San Francisco
in 1847, but for the *Vincennes* the great ocean was an old
story. Over one-half of her years had already been spent
there. On her maiden voyage from 1826 to 1830 she felt
the pulse of an American trade at Canton involving fifty
American ships a year and eight million dollars. In 1833,
the year of her second Pacific cruise, 392 American whaling
ships carried ten thousand men into the Pacific with outfits
valued at twelve million dollars. On her third Pacific adventure as flagship for the expedition under Lt. Charles
Wilkes, she helped chart hundreds of reefs and rocks and
shoals which loomed more and more perilous as American
shipping moved more widely over the great ocean. In 1846,
on her fourth cruise to the Pacific, she brought plucky old
Commodore James Biddle in an unsuccessful try to unseal
the commercial riches of Japan. In 1850 the *Vincennes*
sailed the Pacific again and, while anchored in San Francisco Bay in the newest state of the Union, she lost many
of her crew to a gold mania which had already awakened
in millions a new interest in the Pacific.

By 1850, with the added attractions of California and
gold, Congress showed awareness of Pacific expansion as
never before. Ned was still in the Southwest finishing his
work with Captain Pope when Congress prompted the Navy
to send another mission to open Japan. But Ned had been

1. Charles S. Stewart, *A Visit to the South Seas, 1* (2 vols. New York, 1831),
140, called the *Vincennes* "the most beautiful vessel of her class, and the
fastest sailer in our navy."

back home in Philadelphia for some months when, in March 1852, the Navy recalled its first choice for the job, Commodore John H. Aulick, and placed in his stead Matthew Calbraith Perry.

In July 1853, the Great Commodore, like Manifest Destiny incarnate, churned his paddlewheels into Tokyo Bay. The first night "the towering ships slept motionless on the water, and the twinkling lights of the towns along the shore went out one by one. A few beacon fires lighted on the hilltops, the rattling cordage of an occasional passing junk, the musical tones of a distant temple bell that came rippling over the bay at intervals through the night—these were to us the only tokens of life in the sleeping empire."[2] For two centuries Japan had turned its eyes inward, executing citizens who escaped and returned, imprisoning strangers who landed on its soil. Now it awoke to the two-fisted spirit of Matthew Perry and found itself agreeing, "with sincere and cordial amity," to receive American ships at Shimoda and Hakodate for provisions and for exchange of goods, to assist shipwrecked crews, and eventually to admit United States agents at the two treaty ports.

But what good was a treaty if ships could not find the harbors or continually raked their hulls on unknown reefs? There were no accurate charts of Japanese coasts, not by standards of the day. An 1823 engraved map of Nippon had been smuggled out by the Dutch during their period of exclusive trade privileges, but for navigation it was about as useful as one of the early Spanish maps had been for travel in the Far West. The American West and the far Pacific were in many ways analogous. They each contained treasures beckoning to Americans—California minerals, Oregon soil, or Japanese trade—but the routes were vague and ill-defined. As Ned Kern once helped Frémont and the Topographical Corps mark trails in the American West, so he

2. John S. Sewall, *Logbook of the Captain's Clerk* (Bangor, Me., 1905), pp. 145–46.

now was to help the Navy chart the whole world of waters
and islands between San Francisco and China.

And if, as Kern had already demonstrated, botany and
zoology and meteorology reaped rich rewards during the
mapping of the West, so too they would be prime objects in
his new work. One purpose of the expedition was to extend
the body of learning to complete the vast catalogue of the
earth's plants and animals, a great dream of nineteenth-
century science. Darwin had dreamed it as he watched the
Beagle cut the waves twenty years earlier. The scientists
with Charles Wilkes had dreamed it ten years before.
Wherever there were scientific academies or even amateur
collectors the dream was dreamed. The North Pacific Expedition included four pure scientists, not counting the
astronomers and surgeons and draughtsmen, whose normal
naval duties could be supplemented by more specifically
scientific ones. Charles Wright, the botanist, was probably
the most distinguished of the savants. He had spent years
tramping over the American Southwest, identifying new
species of cactus and, meanwhile, developing a serious im-
pairment of vision and a hypersensitive disposition. But
personality aside, he had characteristics remarkably like Edward Kern: "a love of nature, an eagerness to discover new
things, an impatience of physical idleness, an overmastering
love of travel."[3] The chief zoologist was William Stimpson,
a protégé of Louis Agassiz, whom Wright described as going
into ecstasy over "a nearly shapeless mass of jelly or some
ugly worm that any one else would shudder to touch."[4] And
then there was Kern himself, a member of the Academy of
Natural Sciences—not only an artist of the expedition but
assigned to be taxidermist as well.

So the North Pacific Exploring Expedition had been officially created with a Congressional blessing of $125,000

3. Samuel W. Geiser, *Naturalists of the Frontier* (Dallas, 1937), p. 220.
4. C. Wright to A. Gray, April 9, 1854, Gray Herbarium, Harvard University.

three months before Perry sailed. The Navy gave the overall command to Cadwalader Ringgold, a rigid disciplinarian, who hoisted his flag on the U.S.S. *Vincennes.* Ringgold was to have trouble in the days ahead. He seemed adept at alienating his officers and the scientists. He was unpredictable: several times on the voyage, without any warning, he ordered the expedition to sea while the ships were unprepared and the scientists in the midst of delicate observations. The scientists came to distrust him and wrangling grew frequent.⁵ But this was all in the future.

For the first days the seas were heavy, but the little squadron of five ships carried all possible canvas—studding sails billowing taut on both sides below and aloft. Scientific work began immediately—rain gauges were set, lines and reels wound for deep-sea soundings, kegs rigged for measuring currents, chronometers synchronized for the entire squadron and thereafter compared every Saturday. Day after day as the ships moved east, the scientists gathered with excitement over each new bit of information, were it nothing more than a sea-borne oil cask, worm-eaten and overlaid with barnacles and crustaceans. Birds, seaweed, fish, eclipses, halos of the moon—all were carefully observed. Hygrometers, barometers, thermometers—some in the masthead, some on deck, some in the sea—all were dutifully chronicled. Even on the Fourth of July amid special luncheons for the officers and a liquid "splicing of the main brace" for the men, the chief event for the scientists was dredging up "a crab of prism form, displaying all the colors of the rainbow but no larger than a pea."⁶

5. Henry K. Stevens, Journal, 1853–55, entry Oct. 21, 1853; Jonathan Carter, Journal, 1853–56 (Private), entries Sept. 27 and Oct. 5, 1853; both in Navy Branch, National Archives. For Stimpson and Wright's connection with Ringgold's insanity, see C. Wright to A. Gray, April 9 and 12, 1854, Gray Herbarium, Harvard University.

6. Frederick Stuart, Journal, 1853–1854, entry July 4, 1853, Navy Branch, National Archives.

Edward was called upon to sketch specimens, faithfully to delineate feathers and fins and follicles. He worked under William Brenton Boggs, associate of the National Academy of Design and an artist who, in search of a living, had joined the Navy and now served as purser, in addition to artist, for the Ringgold expedition. When he was not drawing, Ned helped the naturalists stuff or bottle specimens, and he might gratefully have remembered the advice of his old friend Drayton to learn a little taxidermy before leaving with Frémont. As a naturalist, he drew upon eight years of experience, most of them in the field, and he now began several collections of his own—shells and sea life of various kinds.

As artist of the expedition, he was also "photographist," in charge of a mass of daguerreotype apparatus—thirty-six dozen plates, glass coverings, containers with chemicals, mercury, hyposulfite of soda, chloride of gold, buffing sticks, sponges, coating boxes, even two headrests. On the Frémont third expedition, as we have seen, Ned's opportunity to practice photography had not materialized. Now, eight years later, with customary bravado, he agreed to handle the photographic work still without knowing a great deal about it. Though he had experimented with daguerreotypes after his return from New Mexico, on his appointment to the North Pacific Expedition he expressed to Ringgold his hope that the supplies could be procured early to give him a "better opportunity of becoming acquainted with the art."[7] Three times Ringgold sent him to New York at Navy expense to buy and to learn from the firm of Edward and Henry Anthony. And he carried close at hand Henry Hunt Snelling's manual, *The Art of Photography,* from

7. E. Kern to C. Ringgold, Jan. 24, 1853, Navy Branch, National Archives. See also R. Kern to E. Kern, May 2, 1852, Huntington Library; S. F. Baird to C. Ringgold, Nov. 19, 1852, Archives of the Smithsonian Institution.

which he probably learned most of what he knew. Of course, the whole field of photography was only fourteen years old (since Daguerre had announced his process). American painters like Samuel F. B. Morse or John Mix Stanley were only beginning to express interest in the new medium, and scientific expeditions were only gradually becoming aware of an invaluable tool. Edward followed very closely behind the first pioneers in documentary photography.[8]

Onward the five ships sailed, latter-day *Beagles* pursuing a scientific star—Madeira, Simonstown, Good Hope, Sydney, Guam, to China. Such was the route of the *Vincennes* and the *Porpoise*. The three other ships sailed more directly, like the China clippers, by Java Head through the Gaspar Straits into the China Sea. But always on all decks and bridges ran the endless observations, readings, surveys. Looking over the charts, one of the lieutenants pictured the continuous line of deep-sea soundings following them from ocean to ocean as an endless trail like the Milky Way.[9] But the work did not run happily. Young Lt. John Brooke, who had begun the voyage with the deepest admiration for Ringgold, now resolved simply to keep out of the way of his commander. "It makes me despondent," he wrote, "to look around and see the universal dissatisfaction. I never saw

8. The full title of the Snelling book was *The History and Practice of the Art of Photography* (New York, 1849); Edward probably used the 4th edition of 1853. With Perry's expedition, Eliphalet Brown, Jr., fresh from employment with Currier and Ives, had set up his camera in the temples of Okinawa and Japan. Matthew Perry, *Narrative of the Expedition, 1* (Washington, 1856), 154; Edward McCauley, *With Perry in Japan* (Princeton, 1942), p. 110. On western land expeditions the credit for the first use of photography usually goes either to John Mix Stanley, who took daguerreotypes on the Stevens survey for the Pacific Railroad, or to Solomon N. Carvalho, who photographed Frémont's fifth expedition. Both of these men left the settlements in 1853, the same year Edward sailed on the North Pacific expedition. Their experiments were all preceded, however, by Frémont's use of a daguerreotype on his first expedition, 1842.

9. Alexander W. Habersham, *My Last Cruise* (Philadelphia, 1857), p. 495.

anything like it."[10] And withal, Kern was on hand, his pencils ready for headlands and islands, water colors for vegetation and clouds, camera for the people and more important harbors; but he, too, came to avoid Ringgold whenever possible.

In March 1854, as Perry's squadron lay in Tokyo Bay about to consummate the final treaty with Japan, the *Vincennes* reached Hong Kong. While Edward watched the coast of China rise, he might have seen the smoke of burning villages—fires from the T'ai P'ing Rebellion, one of those periodic native revulsions against the Occidental intruder. Finding most of the American East India Squadron off in Japan with Perry, Commander Ringgold became frightened for the lives and property of American citizens around Canton. Although such was not his responsibility, he took the protection of American merchants on his own shoulders and held the North Pacific Exploring Expedition in the Hong Kong–Canton area.

Some of the officers became more and more restive under their commander. They began to notice a peculiar quality in Ringgold's fear: his customary touch of martinet was growing pre-eminent. Instead of sending the ships to sea without preparation, as he had done at Simon's Bay, he now ordered endless repairs and reconditionings, and, when finished, the same repairs would be reordered on the same ships—a kind of "monomania" as Brooke called it. When Perry returned to China in August, the expedition still rode anchor at Hong Kong and still underwent repairs.

The affairs of the Ringgold group presented a rather sorry picture to the returning Perry. Before Hong Kong, nine months of hard work lay behind the explorers—long hours of soundings and tidal observations, sometimes in

10. As quoted in George M. Brooke, Jr., "John Mercer Brooke, Naval Scientist," Ph.D. dissertation, University of North Carolina, 1955, p. 339; hereafter cited as Brooke, "Brooke."

small cramped launches; hiking over headlands for sightings from the theodolite; tedious nights by telescopes, watching for culminations of moon and stars. Then had followed months of waiting at Hong Kong. As July and August came on, insufferable heat descended, bringing restless nights of trying to sleep on deck, days of listening to the tar melting from the rigging drop by drop on the awnings. And sickness, boils, fevers. Ned made a few trips to nearby Canton and sketched what he could of a city in rebellion—the hong merchants, the execution yard with piles of decomposing heads, the delicate *Flying Cloud* resting off Whampoa. Given Ned's propensities for a good time, it is probable that he joined in a few brawls, for liquor had a hand in disrupting the health, morale, and discipline of the expedition. But most calamitous of all, Commander Ringgold took ill with malaria, or "intermittent fever," as it was described, suffering chills, raging fever, periods of delirium. Perry reported the expedition "in a state of confusion," and John Rodgers, second in command under Ringgold, wrote, "The officers were disheartened, out of temper and disgusted . . . everything was out of joint."[11]

On the night of July 24—the weather hot, the commander ill and irritable—the surgeon of the expedition, William Grier, committed some minor breach of discipline, the exact nature of which has not been recorded. Ringgold punished him in a way which even the commander later admitted "was probably harsher than the occasion required." Grier thereupon notified Lt. Rodgers that Commander Ringgold's illness had assumed "the form of mental alienation," with "some reason to fear it may prove permanent." Rodgers informed Perry. The Commodore made a few informal investigations and then convoked a medical board to examine Ringgold. The board pronounced him

11. M. Perry to C. Dobbin, Aug. 9, 1854, Navy Branch, National Archives; J. Rodgers to F. Maury, March 5, 1855, Library of Congress.

insane; Perry removed him from command and ordered him home.[12]

Ringgold on his last day in China received from his crew a letter of affection and farewell, then with a medical escort he left his ship, a broken man.[13] Perry placed Lt. John Rodgers in command of the expedition.

Kern now watched the squadron convulse under a major change. For months during the Ringgold derangement officers had been making charges and countercharges against one another. The new commander ceased all repairs while he shuffled officers and crew. Alexander Habersham, an opinionated and verbose lieutenant who later wrote a rambling account of his experiences on the expedition, described the weeks as "nothing but change—change—change." Kern, however, was not moved from the *Vincennes*. He had avoided the spats among the regular Navy men, and in any case his bulky daguerreotype supplies precluded any too precipitate orders to move him about.

12. The quotation of Ringgold is from his *Memorial, . . . to the Congress of the United States* (Washington, 1856), pp. 11–12; of Rodgers, from Ringgold's *Defence . . . before Court of Inquiry* (Washington, 1857), p. 7. See also William Grier, Journal, entries of July 24 and 25, Aug. 1, 1854, Navy Branch, National Archives. Ringgold later admitted that he was ill, that the climate was enough to drive anyone to distraction, that the morphine and opium prescriptions probably affected his mental stability. But he contended that the medical board had labeled him permanently insane after no more than a morning's chit-chat over a glass of wine. "If its object had been to ascertain whether a barrel of beef was sound or unsound, it could not have been marked by more carelessness and irregularity." (Ringgold, *Memorial*, p. 19; and *Defence*, p. 11). Temporary illness, which he maintained was the only trouble, was not sufficient cause for outright recall from command. Behind the affair, he claimed, was Perry's vindictiveness, aroused by earlier disagreements between the two men. However pleased Perry might have been at the chance, the medical inquiry gave him sufficient excuse to act.

13. Ringgold, *Defence*, p. 30; H. Stevens, Journal, Sept. 21, 1854. A Naval Retirement Board later placed Ringgold on inactive service. Recovered in mind and body, he spent years lashing back at Perry and the implications of the removal, until he was restored to positions of command in 1857, just in time for meritorious service in the Civil War.

Commander John Rodgers was a man of the sea from a long line of midshipmen, commodores, and rear admirals. His stern, storm-gray eyes and his broad shoulders suggested an independent spirit. Now forty-two, he had served the Navy since he was sixteen; before his assignment with Ringgold, he had finished three years with the Coast Survey under his good friend Alexander Dallas Bache. Deeply interested in science, Rodgers thoroughly enjoyed his work on the North Pacific expedition.[14]

One of his first acts as commander was to reduce the squadron to four ships: the flagship *Vincennes,* still bearing Edward Kern; the smaller, two-masted *Porpoise;* the even smaller schooner *Fenimore Cooper;* and the bulky *John Hancock,* the only steamship of the expedition. The *John Kennedy* was detached from the expedition and stationed near Canton. The *Hancock* and the *Cooper* were needed on a diplomatic mission to North China to defend, as Wright described them, a few "purse-proud effeminate denationalized dime-grasping Anglo-Saxons."[15] For the other two ships it was too near the stormy months to tackle the main job in the northern Pacific. Anywhere they went, of course, they would face rough weather, but further waiting would be fatal to morale, so orders went out to the *Vincennes* and the *Porpoise* for an interim survey between southern Japan and Loo Choo (now Okinawa). "We chose

---

14. For Rodgers' life see J. Russell Soley, "Rear-Admiral John Rodgers," *U.S. Naval Institute Proceedings, 8* (1882), pp. 251–65; Asaph Hall, "Biographical Memoir of John Rodgers," National Academy of Sciences, *Biographical Memoirs, 6* (Washington, 1909), pp. 83–92; *Dictionary of American Biography;* for Rodgers' weight see Rodgers to his brother, March 23, 1856, Rodgers Papers, Library of Congress; for Rodgers' feelings regarding Ringgold see Allan B. Cole, ed., *Yankee Surveyors, in the Shogun's Seas: Records of the United States Surveying Expedition to the North Pacific Ocean, 1853–1856* (Princeton, 1947), p. 157.

15. C. Wright to A. Gray, Aug. 12, 1854, Gray Herbarium, Harvard University.

storms rather than disease and enervation," wrote Rodgers to his friend Maury.[16]

Thus in October of 1854 Ned ate sweet potatoes and green turtles on the Bonin Islands (which include Iwo Jima), while he helped in the collecting and the triangulations. *(Fig. 46)* In November the *Vincennes* doubled back to Loo Choo *(Figs. 44, 45)*, the central pendant in the chain that dips from southern Japan to Formosa. Here Ned set up his daguerreotype and proceeded to film the civilization which Perry had visited four months earlier.[17] Perry had forced a treaty on the fourteen-year-old reigning prince of Okinawa, a guarantee to provide American ships with provisions. Now Rodgers found the Okinawans evading his requests for beef and vegetables and wood. Kern packed his daguerreotype for a march on the palace. About a hundred men, all armed and drawing a field cannon, marched in ranks over the paved streets and out three miles through sweet-potato fields to the stone palace walls. The officers and Ned went through a portal "for Receiving the Gods," and there high officials brought them pipes and tobacco and served them saki, tea, and cakes. Rodgers presented the grievances; Okinawan officials proffered apologies and assurances. Aboard ship that night, Ned watched long lines of men bearing wood to the shore. The show had worked; the treaty had been enforced.

Onward they went, surveying, charting, sketching along the Ryukyus, the string of islands through which the California clippers veered to China, until Ned had his first view of the coast of Japan, the extreme southern tip leading into the Bay of Kagoshima. The surveyors immediately cast calculating eyes on a peak near the headlands from which a score of islands to the south could be triangulated. It was a strategic position, as Pilot Peak or Fontaine qui

16. April 5, 1855, Naval Foundation Papers, Library of Congress.

17. J. Rodgers, Journal, 1854, Naval Foundation Papers, Library of Congress.

Bouit had been to Frémont. But this was Japanese soil. Perry's treaty said American ships could land at Shimoda and Hakodate, but at other places only in dire emergencies. Any local official, steeped in laws against foreigners, could fear, and not without reason, that an American landing might mean loss of his job, if not his head. These particular village leaders brought out a pitiful drawing of a ship in full rig and blew into the sails to indicate how happy they would be if the *Vincennes* got out. But the Japanese, unlike the Americans, were unarmed; the peak stood in the background, solid as a bench mark, and the theodolites were in their cases and ready.

Furthermore, Rodgers was constructing a brief in international law. How could a treaty grant refuge to ships in distress if it did not at the same time imply the right of the distressed to accurate charts? How, without such charts, could a searching captain find the ports of safety and avoid the perils? "To tell a friend," Rodgers wrote the Japanese, "that he might enter the nearest harbor in case his vessel were sinking or on fire or dismasted or the crew starving, but to hide from him the position of the harbor, and the way to enter it, would seem more like mockery than good faith."[18] Japanese swords were raised in Kagoshima Bay, and cordons drawn, but they gave in at the brandishing of American guns, and the survey went on. Ashore, Ned helped Lt. John Brooke, the astronomer, in his observation and watched him impress the natives by a lucky shot of a small bird at seventy yards. Kern also drew the headlands, dredged some unusual crabs from the harbor, laughed in the wardroom at stories of dunking arrogant Japanese guards, and teased his mind over the problems of communicating with the Japanese holding only a Chinese dictionary.

In January and February of 1855 the squadron rendezvoused in Hong Kong—or more accurately, three ships

18. Cole, ed., *Yankee Surveyors*, p. 49.

rendezvoused in Hong Kong while one rested at the bottom of the sea. The *Vincennes* came, followed by the *Hancock* and the *Cooper,* but the *Porpoise* with her eighty men never returned. Through the Taiwan Straits the *Vincennes* had lost sight of her in a driving mist; then had waited through a typhoon and searched strait after strait, port after port, for some sign or some word. The loss of the *Porpoise* remained the great tragedy of the expedition.

Now reduced to three ships, the survey prepared for its major northward task, and in April sailed from Hong Kong amidst a Chinese farewell of exploding firecrackers. On May 13 the *Vincennes* splashed its anchors into the Bay of Shimoda, just south of Tokyo Bay. At least the expedition now lay in an official treaty port and the dredgings and triangulations would seem less like stolen fruit than they had at Kagoshima. Work went forward briskly. The rocks in the harbor were carefully charted and checked against Perry's surveys, crustaceans were lifted from tidal pools, birdsnest ferns and native camellias were dried and pressed.

For two weeks Ned drank in the exoticism of Shimoda. His sketches and water colors trembled with curiosity: temples and tea houses and blind priests begging. With the other officers, he reveled in a bazaar specially set up for the Americans—silks, block prints, porcelains, lacquerware, birds of gold enameling. "Of what use?" the Americans frowned—and purchased by the handful. There were exchange rate problems, but Ned bought, thinking of the house on Filbert Street, the opening of boxes, the regaling of the family with stories.

Rodgers, meanwhile, wanted a showdown on his right to survey the entire Japanese coast. He delivered to the governors of Shimoda a long letter addressed to the "Honourable Secretary of State," reiterating his Kagoshima interpretation of international law: "the arguments I use are necessity, our treaty, your friendship, and the natural right

which every nation has, . . . to examine hidden dangers. . . .
I dare not anticipate the consequences of refusal."[19]

His letter was never answered. The Shimoda governors
were unwilling to grant any special privileges and even
denied Rodgers' petition to send a ship on a visit to Heda,
a very few miles to the northwest. But Rodgers, believing
as he did that "words without the authority of many cannon
will avail little," sent the *Hancock* off to Heda, and that was
that. Rodgers was aware of his position as the first American
official to deal with the Japanese since the final ratifications
of the Perry treaty. Knowing Perry's injunction, "One rash
man may overturn all that has been accomplished," Rodgers
took care never to be rude.[20] But he could not risk an attack
on his survey, and he now openly and purposefully made
plans to carry through an idea he had earlier entertained—
a detailed charting of the rocky, storm-lashed, 450-mile
Japanese coast between the two treaty ports, Shimoda and
Hakodate. The governors of Shimoda refused permission.
Rodgers ignored them and called for volunteers to man a
four-ton open launch on a dangerous job. Ned Kern was
hardly one to miss such an opportunity.

On May 28 Ned gathered pencils, a few colors, pads, a
change of clothing, and climbed with the eleven other volunteers into the launch. Nicknamed the "Vincennes Junior," she had a light forecastle and a poop covering a few
lockers and provisions for two weeks and was rigged as a
sloop, spreading 160 square yards of canvas. Since the gunwale ran only fourteen inches above water, canvas weather-
cloth was roped to eighteen-inch stanchions along the rails.
A mounted twelve-pound howitzer, carbines, pistols, and
cutlasses provided protection of another sort. And hoping
the guns would not need to be used, there was a gift supply
—fishhooks, colored cloth, brass buttons—much as if the

19. Ibid., p. 51.
20. Perry, *Narrative*, p. 17; Cole, ed., *Yankee Surveyors*, pp. 45, 61.

ship were going into western Indian country.[21]

In charge was Lt. John M. Brooke, a man whom Kern had come to know and respect as well as he once had Frémont. Not yet thirty, this dark-haired, bearded, cigar-smoking Southerner was as active as Ned, an expert swimmer and fencer, but he was moody and reflective. His luminous, penetrating eyes were clues to his interest in mesmerism and clairvoyance. Like Rodgers he had labored for the Coast Survey under Alexander Dallas Bache and had worked at the Naval Observatory with Matthew Maury. Indeed, his work with Maury had resulted in a major contribution to naval science—the Brooke deep-sea sounding-lead, a vastly improved device for measuring depths and taking samples of the ocean bottom. Without it the Atlantic Cable could not have been laid when it was, and on it much of Maury's deep-sea work rested. Although Brooke's reflective moodiness was a departure from Ned's good-humored openness, the two had much in common—scientific skills and interests and zeal for sketching and painting.[22]

The three ships drew away from the launch, each on a separate route, to meet in Hakodate, 450 miles north, in three weeks. Strong north winds and a rough sea promised anything but a pleasure jaunt. Low clouds obscured the shore, and after sailing ten or twelve miles in rain and spindrift, the launch's crew pulled into a sheltered cove and made camp for the night. The firm land and a hot fire raised spirits and warmed skins.

Seven men slept on shore. They had no legal right to do so—not by Japanese law, not by the Perry treaty, and

21. For good description of launch see John Brooke, "Coasting in Japan," *U.S. Nautical Magazine and Naval Journal*, 5 (1856), p. 197. Brooke, "Brooke," p. 422, gives total number of men in launch as fifteen.

22. Maury to Rodgers, Jan. 17, 1855; Maury to Ringgold, Nov. 14, 1853; Navy Branch, National Archives. I am indebted to Dr. George M. Brooke, Jr., for help in describing John Brooke and for permission to read his unpublished dissertation, previously cited (Brooke, "Brooke"). In the latter, see especially pp. 38, 86, 142–48, 179, 211.

certainly not by any special permission. Just before midnight officers from Shimoda carrying paper lanterns raised the sleepers and told them they must get back to the boat, that this was not a treaty port. Yawning and pretending sleep, the seamen turned over and ignored the disturbance. The chief functionary gesticulated to no avail, worked himself into a rage, knocked his fist through his lantern, and stalked off. At daybreak Brooke talked with the officials, now somewhat calmer, who continued to protest of the launch's cruise, "It is not in the treaty." But the launch sailed early that morning.

South winds swept the "Vincennes Junior" across the Sagami Sea around Oshima, a volcanic crater jutting from the waters, till they saw the sun set beyond the entrance to Tokyo Bay. Next morning in the Bay of Susaki, a small harbor opening to the west just outside Tokyo Bay, they took triangulations southward across the Sagami Sea, connecting observations with those made at Shimoda. That afternoon weather forced them into a rocky inlet dotted with fishing boats. Primitive fishermen's shacks crowded the shores, and a small temple stood precariously on the brow of a steep rock looking seaward—God of the Sea protecting those who go down to the sea, a shrine to Poseidon, a Seamen's Bethel. By the time the Americans landed on the beach under the temple rock, a crowd of a thousand made it hard to find footage ashore. They were sociable and friendly villagers, letting the Americans wander at will into their houses of sliding-paneled walls.

Curiosity overcame any fears of white skin or of official disfavor: first the younger, bolder spirits, then the older people surrounded Kern and the others, examining their clothing, taking pulse beats, and feeling beards and bodies. In a decorously veiled reference to obvious human relationships, Brooke commented, "Nor were the females less forward than the men in these investigations; it seemed that they would not have hesitated to admit us as members of their families."[23] Since even the reserved Brooke observed, "the young girls were engaging in their manners and some of them were singularly beautiful," he was probably wise to order all hands to sleep that night aboard the launch.

Ned sketched all the harbors. One line drawing of Utsiura, with another temple on a headland, another throng, and the launch in the midst of larger fishing boats, he redid in full water colors, apparently feeling some fondness for the spot. Perhaps this partiality was piqued by a young girl with jet-black hair, expressive eyes, dark lashes, and graceful bare limbs whom the Americans surprised while, like Rebecca, she filled a porcelain bottle at a spring. Along the whole coast the fishermen, with muscular bodies naked except for a loin cloth, made fine models for action sketches.

Not all the nights were spent on shore or in harbors. Whenever the barometer fell and the clouds piled up on the southwestern horizon, the "Vincennes Junior" headed away from the lee shore, seeking the relative safety of an open sea. One such time, seven days out from Shimoda and a long way from any harbor, rain and scud began whipping frantically in a strong northeaster. The men huddled behind the weather cloth, watching the barometer descend mercilessly. By three in the afternoon the sea swells reared higher than the masthead. But the waves only curled jaggedly not yet completely breaking, and Brooke kept the mainsail set, heading for deeper water. The gunwale often ran below the sea; thank God for the tight cloth. The tiller cracked. Then at the top of a wild watery hill before careening down again, just off the weather bow, a great white bank of foam shot high in the air. Breakers! Rocks beneath! The mainsail was quickly reefed, the helm put down to weather a shock. But no oncoming wave, no wall of surf, only the same roaring winds and peaked waters. There, where all eyes had been riveted on danger, turned the slip-

23. Cole, ed., *Yankee Surveyors*, p. 89; Brooke, "Coasting in Japan," 5, 283.

pery black hump of a whale spuming a jet high into the wind. On his back the sea had broken.

That night of desperate hauling away from the shore was only one of many, in rains and gales and thick mists. It was a dangerous coast and a stormy one, but the work went on. Not many hours after the whale scare, when by midnight the winds and sea had somewhat abated, the men cast the lead and duly recorded no bottom at thirty-nine fathoms. There were compensating hours of rare beauty; one night while the launch was forcing itself off a hazardous headland, Ned was awakened before a wondrously luminous sea beneath a lowering sky. It was the loveliest phosphorescence he had ever seen.

There were also pleasantly isolated nights in quiet coves with waterfalls of clear water and sandy beaches. And there were others, like that in the Bay of Sendai, with thousands of eager Japanese swarming about them. A hundred scenes remained vivid in Ned's mind—the kindly and generous Nipponese fisherman, "Captain Rice," standing motionlessly dejected when they had no more room for his hampers of rice and fish; the furnace of a primitive salt factory before which their jackets steamed while drying; blind beggars on the shore at Isokona facing the launch for hours as if hoping to absorb an impression of these bearded strangers.

The Americans must have amazed the Japanese, and Ned's practical joking contributed. One day they spotted a fishing junk silently at anchor in the open sea, all quiet; apparently the entire crew was catching an early afternoon nap. The Americans steered close, almost touching her gunwales, and Ned cupped his hands and let out a shriek, straight from the Navajo. "No war-whoop ever rang through the air more piercingly, nor roused a startled sleeper more suddenly than his wild yell."[24] The Americans laughed for days, remembering the petrified faces which shortly peered

24. Brooke, "Coasting in Japan," 5, 412.

out. At other times Ned's capering was the center of delighted attention. He crowed like a cock for one group of natives,
and they were captivated, laughing so hard that they kept
him crowing till he swore he could crow no more.

The last headland, the final observation off Cape Shiriya,
the dash across the Sangar Straits to the bay of Hakodate,
and they had finished their twenty-one days of labor at
eleven o'clock on the evening of June 17. In the harbor
among the junks slowly emerged the lights and shape of
their mother *Vincennes* and her two sister ships. "We heard
the sound of many feet, and the words 'the launch, the
launch has come!' "[25] After a few days the little craft was
hauled back on deck, and for weeks her crew retold and
embellished—Ned, for one, would never underplay a story
—the tales of storm and danger.

Ten days at Hakodate (the seamen called it "Hack-your-
daddy") were enough for fresh supplies, coal which had
been sent ahead for the *Hancock*'s boilers, and more tiffs
with local Japanese officials. Ned's impressions of Hakodate,
the last Japanese city he saw, were preserved in a sheaf of
water colors and sketches—interiors of the unusually expansive temples, and a gloomy cemetery arched with dark pines
like the virgin forests of western Pennsylvania.

By now he had a rather high but nevertheless limited respect for the Japanese. He would not stoop, as some American seamen had done, to defiling a shrine near the entrance
to Hakodate harbor. And Edward, like most Americans in
these first contacts, preferred the Japanese people to the
Chinese, probably because the chief contact with the Chinese was through the crusted filth of Canton. But even the
Japanese, Edward would agree, were peculiar, primitive,
and in some ways barbaric. Take, for example, the custom
of mixing the sexes without shame in the public baths—a

25. Brooke, "Coasting in Japan," 6 (1857), 37–38, as quoted in Brooke,
"Brooke," 438. Arrival date from Log of *Vincennes*, Navy Branch, National
Archives; Stevens' Journal says launch arrived June 16.

situation Ned sketched. As Habersham wrote, "it must be remembered that they are half-civilized Orientals, and heathens at that. . . . They bathe promiscuously with the opposite sex in the public baths, because, I suppose, their ancestors did so before them, and their primitive ideas recognize no harm in so doing." Or take the Japanese use of soft, disposable paper for handkerchiefs; Ned probably joined the other Americans in labeling this a laughable, primitive custom. Rodgers epitomized the attitude of frowning condescension: "In Japan, China, and Loo Choo, as in Europe, poor Truth lives in a well."[26]

The squadron, wrote Habersham, "now began to show the effects of hard work and heavy weather. The ships looked rusty, our boats were bruised and battered, and we ourselves looked miserably seedy and overworked." Beyond Hakodate the three ships took different routes. The *Hancock*, with Lieutenant Habersham keeping his gossipy notes, circled the Sea of Okhotsk. Here in this upstairs back room of the Pacific, in the "scattering and streetless" port of Ayan, in uninhabited bays of the Shantar Islands, everywhere, the *Hancock* found whalers, sometimes crowds of them, watering their ships or gathering wild rhubarb by streams in spruce forests. The *Hancock*'s careful survey of these coasts would hardly go unused. The little *Cooper* meanwhile surveyed the whole Aleutian chain and searched for survivors or news of the *Monongahela,* only the most recent whaleship lost in the uncharted reaches of these North Pacific seas.

But the flagship with Ned Kern aboard took an even more daring track—northward toward Bering Straits and Arctic seas into a region of fogs, milky mists, the hearts of storms, or of cruelly calm and frigid seas. The fogs were the worst. The Russians at Petropavlovsk smiled at their surveying plans, knowing that vessels had cruised for seasons

26. The earlier Habersham quote is from *My Last Cruise,* p. 241. J. Rodgers to M. Maury, April 5, 1855, Naval Foundation Papers, Library of Congress.

without making a single significant sighting of sun or soil. Rodgers had anticipated such trouble, and as early as Hong Kong he had envisioned setting a small party ashore along the entrance of Bering Straits to observe for absolute longitude and magnetic declination and all those things which fogs and motion might hinder at sea.

As the *Vincennes* moved under thick skies toward Bering Straits, Rodgers ordered Brooke, his lieutenant of the launch venture, to prepare a landing party. It was to stay ashore for an indefinite period while the ship went on into the Arctic. Again Ned Kern stepped forward, an eager volunteer. Others to go were William Stimpson and Charles Wright, the naturalists; three seamen; Micalaus, a bearded old Cossack taken on at Petropavlovsk who knew the native tongue; and three marines for extra protection—eleven men in all.[27]

Northwest of St. Lawrence Island, the ship nosed its way through fog into the narrow Seniavine Strait between Kayne Island and the Siberian mainland. It was a gloomy day and quiet, with land near but none sighted through the drifting fog bank; small boats were sent ahead. Suddenly the mist rose, and from deck Kern saw a desolate stretch of long, level peninsula protecting a small bay, Glazenap Harbor, which boasted only a few moundlike native huts and piles of bleaching whale bones.

Out from shore paddled about seventy-five natives, Chukchi Indians, in round skin boats. Ned and the landing party had been briefed on the Chukchis, a fiercely independent tribe which, like the Navajo, doggedly fought white infiltration. Since the early eighteenth century they had held the extreme northeast corner of Siberia from Russian advances, refusing tribute to the Czars, checkmating expeditions, occasionally accepting temporary defeat only to boil up anew against the invaders. Some of the Chukchis lived inland as

27. Brooke, Journal, Aug. 5, 1855, as quoted in Brooke, "Brooke," p. 456.

nomads, their life dependent on reindeer herds, and these, fortunately for the landing party, were the most violent. Along the coasts, the Chukchis fared on whale, seal, and walrus, and were often miserably poor, begging from their more truculent kinsmen. But these coastal tribes were nevertheless Chukchis—bold, free, with fine, tall bodies and athletic stance.[28]

Knowing the Chukchis, Rodgers felt considerable anxiety at leaving eleven men alone with them for a month or six weeks. He feared not only for lives, but also for work: the Chukchis had completely frustrated a Russian exploring expedition some sixty years earlier by destroying the surveying outfit and refusing to allow the making of notes or calculations. So Rodgers and Brooke carefully selected the site with protection in mind. At the point on the headland they raised two tents and a more commodious structure made with spars and sails, landed the transit house ("a snug little box of hooks and staples"), the daguerreotype, boxes of instruments, provisions for two months, the howitzer which had sailed on the "Vincennes Junior," carbines, muskets, rifles, and a whaleboat for escape in case the ship did not return. They called it Brookville. Native women and children lent a hand in landing supplies, and apparently convinced Brooke that no trouble need be feared; nevertheless, the peninsula was fortified by running a line of earth-filled barrels and a trench beyond the bastion. "No savages are to be trusted," Rodgers warned Brooke. "All are fickle and revengeful."[29]

Rodgers came ashore for the final farewell. He talked with the native chief, promising him rewards if the party

28. Joseph E. Nourse, *American Explorations in the Ice Zones* (Boston, 1884), pp. 119–20, 120 n.; Frank A. Golder, *Russian Expansion on the Pacific* (Cleveland, 1914), pp. 151, 156, 163–64; Richard J. Bush, *Reindeer, Dogs, and Snow-Shoes* (New York, 1871), pp. 383, 426–29, 435–41; H. H. Bancroft, *Alaska* (San Francisco, 1886), pp. 295–96.

29. J. Rodgers to J. Brooke, Aug. 6, 1855, Navy Branch, National Archives; as quoted in Brooke, "Brooke," p. 458.

were treated well; but severe punishment if it was not. On August 9 the *Vincennes* set its sails and cut through the harbor mists, veering northward toward the Arctic.

For Ned the land respite was delightful, and the weather lightened for a time. The peninsula spread like a small version of the prairies in '45, a meadow thick with grass and rich with blue and yellow flowers opening in the short Siberian summer. There were clouds of mosquitoes, but there were also high mountains rising on the inland side of the bay, with snow still in the hollows and with lakes of ice water. The naturalists hiked immediately to the fields, watching birds and unknown animals. Wright, the botanist, whose temperament was as prickly as the *Opuntia wrightii* named for him, or Stimpson, the zoologist, would bring Kern specimens to sketch. But most of the days were given to astronomical and surveying work—accurately mounting the transit, making observations of Jupiter, careful taking of altitudes, measuring of a base line on the peninsula, triangulations, short trips with the theodolite to nearby islands and peaks. Ned hiked to the top of many a mountain to raise a flag for triangulation, and the field books are full of angles for which "Kern" is "right object" or "left object" or the crown of a peak in a sketch. He also spent long hours at the daguerreotype, he helped Brooke diagnose and care for the sick, and whenever Brooke was away from camp, Kern was left in charge.[30]

He particularly enjoyed drawing the natives, dressed in reindeer, fox, or seal skins under baggy raincoats of whale intestine. In the background he sketched their huts of hide stretched over whalebone, their rude utensils, the ground strewn with moose bones. Like any man so long at sea, he paid special attention to the women. When the Chukchis had first swarmed onto the *Vincennes,* two young girls had

30. Hydrographic Office Field Notebooks, 1855–1939, Navy Branch, National Archives; for Kern as doctor and second in command see Brooke, "Brooke," pp. 465–66.

stayed below in the skin boats. Ned noticed their delicate faces and rather engaging features, asked if he might draw them, and they came aboard. The sailors, sensing an opportunity, offered the girls gifts—needles, beads, and cloth—and they were permitted to go below decks. Brooke said, "The women were most pleased,"[31] and undoubtedly the sailors were too. What favors, if any, Kern received for his sketching, we can only conjecture. But, whatever his purposes, he did try unsuccessfully to get one of the girls to bathe.

On shore he continued his efforts for feminine cleanliness, entreating the girls (including one with "pretty dark eyes") to wash. His comrades dubbed him the "apostle of cleanliness."

"Savage indeed is the man," wrote Brooke, "who is not susceptible to kindness."[32] Something of a camaraderie grew up between the natives and the scientists. The Chukchis taught Ned to capture birds in flight with a sling made of weighted cords. They delighted in showing their skill at running and wrestling, or in imitating the antics of walruses. They particularly enjoyed playing "Hunt the Slipper," a game which the Americans taught them, and many evenings Ned and the sailors would sit with the natives in a close circle, laughing, while the shoe went passing under their knees. They already bore the inevitable marks of the white trader—a mania for tobacco, cravings for brandy and rum, scars from smallpox and syphilis.

Brooke and Kern soon realized that the fiercely independent days of the Chukchis were a thing of the past; at least there was little resentment toward Americans, whatever there might have been toward Russians. The two groups got along beautifully, even to the sharing of an American bowl of hot brandy punch, which on one festive occasion

31. Wilhelm Heine, *Die Expedition in die Seen von China, 3* (3 vols. Leipzig, 1858), 178.
32. Brooke, Journal, as quoted in Brooke, "Brooke," p. 457.

Brooke served to the natives with the philosophic remark,
"Since they know brandy, at least they should learn to drink
it like civilized peoples."[33]

Almost four weeks after the *Vincennes* had disappeared
into the mists, she returned from her bout with Arctic ice.
Rounding the headland, she was greeted with a thirteen-gun
salute from the Brookville howitzer. Three answering sal-
vos, terrifying the Chukchis, boomed across the still Siberian bay.

The *Vincennes* had accomplished valiant and valuable
work, sounding uncharted shoals, dispelling from the charts
non-existent islands, relocating others, tracking to the north
of Wrangel's Land farther than any ship had ever gone. Now
Rodgers greeted his land party warmly, and rewarded the
Chukchis with rice and molasses. Kern and the scientists
brought aboard endless numbers of kegs and cans and bottles, dried plants, Chukchi artifacts, and a library of leather
notebooks, filled with astronomical observations and surveying data. Ned's boxes of daguerreotype plates included
portraits of typical Chukchis, their costumes, and their skin
huts. His sketches filled in where the daguerreotype would
not go, as in the dark interiors of dwellings. There he had
drawn with the same attention to ethnological detail he
had used in California and New Mexico.

The *Vincennes* had a scurvy-ridden crew, with more than
twenty men on the sick list since the beginning of the Arctic
trip. So all possible hands turned to hunting fresh meat or
gathering a few greens, mostly sorrel, from the Glazenap
meadows. The weather had again turned foul with fog and
rain, and on September 17 the *Vincennes* nosed out of Seniavine Strait into the long swells of the Pacific.

Twenty-six days of sailing, through the Aleutians and
southward, and the tired hulk on October 13, 1855—two

33. Heine, *Die Expedition, 3,* 184. "Da sie den Branntwein kennen, so
ist es wenigstens wünschenswerth, dass sie ihn trinken lernen wie civilisirte
Nationen."

years and four months away from American soil—pushed through the Golden Gate to San Francisco and the newly established Navy Yard at Mare Island.

The *Cooper* was already there, and five days later the *Hancock*'s asthmatic boilers and leaky hull came in. The North Pacific Exploring Expedition was reunited for the last time. Rodgers still hoped to extend the labors one more season, charting the merchant routes between San Francisco and China; but as the year 1855 drew to a close, the Secretary of the Navy wrote that the expedition's funds were long since exhausted.

So Rodgers called a general muster on the deck of the *Vincennes,* announced the field work finished, and on behalf of the Navy praised each man for his part. To his superiors he expressed regret that the route to China would not be immediately charted: a proper survey was desperately needed, particularly with talk of a transcontinental railroad. When they could rely on known sea-lanes, American merchants, he prophesied, would carry to Europe by way of San Francisco and New York the teas and silks of the Orient. "We, through California, inherit the trade of the Pacific."[34] It was an old dream—of Timothy Dwight, of Thomas Jefferson, of John Ledyard, and of countless others—and it comes close to expressing the deepest significance of the North Pacific Expedition. The nation which Ned Kern had watched extend itself to its continental borders must now complete the legendary passage to India. Yet the dream had to remain just that for the moment.

Ned relived his earlier good times in San Francisco, but it is doubtful if he recognized the place; the bawdy city grown from gold was hardly the Yerba Buena he had known. Of his old San Francisco friends, Henry King lay buried in the Rockies, and Antoine Robidoux was blind in St. Louis. Pickett was in San Francisco, however, nearly bankrupt but

34. Cole, ed., *Yankee Surveyors,* p. 161.

writing vicious jeremiads and, partly on information earlier received from Ned, about to label Frémont the "humbug nominee of the Black Republicans."[35] McKinstry, disliking the changes the Gold Rush had brought to the north, had moved to San Diego.[36] But John Sutter was still around, and Ned went up the river to the Hock Farm to see him, passing an abandoned, decaying Fort Sutter on the way. Sutter himself was now a poor, bitter man, yet he remembered fondly Ned's bouyant nature, and the two enjoyed their hours of reminiscence and might have had a sad drink in remembrance of Dick, whom Sutter had met on Dick's trip from New Mexico in 1851.

On February 2, 1856, Ned and the *Vincennes* cleared the Golden Gate for the last, tired lap to New York by way of Hawaii. Rodgers thus covered a good part of the survey which officially had been denied him, but the trip was no more than a springboard for future San Francisco–Hawaii surveying. From Honolulu the *Vincennes* swung southward to Tahiti before rounding Cape Horn. During these final months of the cruise Ned amassed a large collection of Sandwich Island shells and added some sprightly Tahitian dancing girls to his sketches.[37] So a brief look at the South Pacific was added to his knowledge of the world before he sailed into the Atlantic and home in July.

35. As quoted in Powell, *Philosopher Pickett*, p. 61.
36. G. McKinstry to E. Kern, Dec. 23, 1851, Fort Sutter Papers.
37. It is possible that on the return voyage Edward did some drawing for Commander Thomas Jefferson Page in the Argentine and Paraguay. During 1853–56 Page was in charge of a Navy expedition along the tributaries of La Plata, and his report of the expedition, *La Plata, the Argentine Confederation, and Paraguay* (New York, 1859), is decorated with woodcuts made from Kern drawings, the originals of which are now in the Thomas Gilcrease Institute, Tulsa, Okla. *(Figs. 51 and 52)*. Whether Edward did these drawings in the field or from sketches provided later in Washington is not revealed by the Log of the *Vincennes*, other records in the National Archives, or the Library of Congress.

CHAPTER 6

The Fenimore Cooper

Once more in Philadelphia, Ned opened his boxes of mementos, and his brothers and sisters must have found the ivories and porcelains even more exotic than the earlier collections from the West. But the excitement of homecoming over, within a short time Ned was settled down in an office in Washington with Rodgers and Brooke facing the organization of a three-year mountain of field notes and drawings. Rodgers described the unfinished state of the sketches: "In consequence of the varying lights, unsteadiness of motion, and inconvenience of place the finer parts could only be indicated; for instance the eyes could not be painted to the figures."[1] To give eyes to his figures, and at the same time help with the charts and reductions, Ned was to receive fourteen hundred dollars a year.

Through 1857 they labored, never forgetting that the last lap of the survey had not actually been finished. Then in

1. J. Rodgers to Navy Department, July 29, 1856, Navy Branch, National Archives.

1858—in another year and on another budget—Rodgers persuaded the Navy Department to allow Brooke to survey the last lap which the North Pacific Expedition had been denied. Brooke's instructions called for determining, between California and China, the positions of islands, shoals, and hazards not properly placed on existing charts. He was to remember that steam was rapidly replacing canvas, and that if steamers were to run along this route, they would need coal depots. Harbors for such purposes he should carefully locate. And, finally, if by chance Brooke were to stumble upon unknown islands with deposits of guano—whitish droppings of sea birds, centuries thick, prized as soil fertilizer—he was to examine such islands well. The survey, said the Secretary of the Navy, could thus aid agriculture as well as commerce.[2]

Brooke, of course, took Ned with him, and in July 1858 the tall Philadelphian and the serious Southerner again walked the booming streets of San Francisco in its Golden Age. They reported to the Mare Island Navy Yard on July 19, the same day the guns saluted the retiring commandant of the yard, David Farragut. Here Brooke and Kern prepared for a job which promised to be more taxing than either the launch's prowl along the Japanese coast or the month of gingerly comradeship with the Chukchis. The route, though well traveled, was not well charted, and over those five thousand miles of water, they and nineteen other men would sail the little U.S.S. *Fenimore Cooper,* ninety-five-ton infant of the earlier expedition.

Inside the bulky sectional dry dock which dominated Mare Island, preparations on the *Cooper* were assiduous and lengthy. The schooner had spent the last two years safely flitting about the harbor on errands for Commandant Farragut, but she now needed her two masts replaced and refittings for sea duty. She was a fast little ship and on the

North Pacific cruise she had been constantly forced to trim sails to keep from brazenly outdistancing the squadron. Brooke and Kern put her astronomical and surveying instruments to interminable tests, often working through whole nights.

As the crew gradually reported for duty, probably the most interesting face for Ned's sketching was that of Joseph Heco. He was one of those Japanese waifs who in the early 1850's wandered through America like spirits stranded in limbo. Heco had been found as a boy, adrift on a storm-battered junk, and taken to San Francisco. In America he made friends and learned English and had even been considered for a part in the Perry negotiations, but Perry's plans for him had miscarried. In Washington during 1858 he met John Brooke and Edward Kern as they were preparing the expedition, and Brooke recognized Heco as a potentially valuable tool in contacts with Japan. He seemed an intelligent and pleasant young man with a serious interest in the project. And, furthermore, he wanted to get home. Brooke signed him on as captain's clerk.[3]

So the *Cooper* caught the winds out of the Golden Gate on September 26, Chinabound on a slow voyage to serve sailor and scientist and perhaps even farmer. For the first three days everyone was seasick, and Brooke commented grimly that the ship acted like a cricket.[4] Thereafter things improved. Ned liked and respected not only his captain, but also the second officer, Lieutenant Charles Thorburn, and Ned himself had personally picked most of the crew. His sketch pads were ready; the instruments stood in good order. Joseph Heco's presence added a certain piquancy, and the proposed treasure-hunt for guano added interest to the voyage.

3. Joseph Heco, *The Narrative of a Japanese,* ed. James Murdoch (n.p., n.d.), pp. 157–83.

4. Brooke, "Brooke," p. 607. Much of the subsequent information is from the Log of the *Fenimore Cooper,* Navy Branch, National Archives.

They worked forty-three long days to Honolulu, but in that time seven rocks or islands, which were reported on the charts as dangers, they determined were no more substantial than mirages. Over some of these "lurking perils," which ships had been detouring for years, Kern helped drag leads up to three miles deep. On one such sounding they pulled a specimen of sea water from three and one-eighth miles, which Brooke believed to be the greatest depth from which water had ever been brought. They measured winds and the distances between waves. They checked magnetic intensities, and they banded the neck of an albatross with latitude, longitude, and date. They charted clouds and rain and asked whalers to do the same in the hope of learning the laws governing Pacific storms. The deep-sea lead got such constant use that twenty-five additional plummets had to be cast in Hawaii.

They spent a month refitting in Honolulu—painting, cleaning tanks, taking on whiskey and candles, soap and pepper—and on December 29 the *Cooper* headed northwest. Between Oahu and Midway a long chain of islets and reefs flecks the sea, and through it the *Cooper* now made its way.

Over the western horizon on January 3 rose a whitish double bulge, like the cranium of a gargantuan whale charging upward. It was the islet of French Frigate Shoals, unclaimed, unoccupied, and covered with guano. The little *Cooper* worked slowly through the encircling reefs and anchored in a cove of the bare rock. Kern rowed ashore with Brooke and some of the men. Thousands of birds rose screaming, and it was hard to walk without stepping on eggs or baby birds. The guano deposits had formed a hard white crust, overlaying deep brown strata, to a depth of over four feet. The total was estimated at about twenty-five thousand tons, enough to gross in the United States a million and a quarter dollars!

Climbing the highest point and shoveling through the

white coating to the volcanic rock, they erected a wooden cross inscribed in black letters on a white background:

> Taken possession of on the 4th of January 1859, by Lieutenant Commanding John M. Brooke, U.S. Schooner Fenimore Cooper, in accordance with Act of Congress passed August 18th, 1856.[5]

They laid a rope from the cross to the cove, which was the only feasible landing spot on the island.

Ned Kern through this little event played a part in the dramatic guano craze of the 1850's. The United States, like almost every other maritime nation, was searching frantically for guano. Worn-out land had been remarkably rejuvenated by its high nitrogen and phosphate content, and in some parts of the agricultural American South, it was looked upon as a magic potion. There were wondrous tales. Boys fell asleep on bags of guano and awoke eight feet tall. Rains fell into guano-laden ships and the masts suddenly sprouted into leafy bowers.

But Peru monopolized the supply. As a result of her foreign borrowings with guano as collateral, an international cartel had grown, and the price in the United States was pushed from forty-five dollars a ton in the 1840's to almost seventy dollars just before the Civil War.

The estimated twenty-five thousand tons on French Frigate Shoals could have become one step in breaking the Peruvian monopoly: that tonnage would have been about one-seventh of the total received by the United States in 1854. Unfortunately the guess was high, and French Frigate Shoals never yielded such a massive bulk of guano. But at

5. J. Brooke to I. Toucey, Feb. 7, 1859, Navy Branch, National Archives; printed in 36th Cong., 1st Sess., Sen. Ex. Doc. 2, pp. 1164–67. Uncertain of proper procedure, Brooke actually acted as a private citizen rather than an officer of the Navy. After their return to Honolulu, Kern, Brooke, and Thorburn went into partnership with a Benjamin F. Snow intending to exploit their claim. For a while they expected to make a fortune, but nothing came of the venture. Brooke, "Brooke," pp. 619 n., 623–25.

least Brooke accurately nailed its position, and Ned Kern's drawing of its white brow circled with hundreds of sea birds graced the report to the Secretary of the Navy.

For another month they moved from reef to atoll to island. They dispelled the notion of the existence of Two Brothers Reef and Neva Island, and they watched the sea break threateningly over Maro Reef though no surface emerged. On Laysan, as Kern and some others were taking observations ashore, a sudden gale ended their explorations and brought them scurrying back to the ship; the seas remained so heavy that the *Cooper* lost an anchor. They sailed to the area north of Lisiansky, but violent squalls made work impossible until it was time for them to return to Honolulu.

It had been a wet and uncomfortable excursion, and two of the crew deserted on the return to Oahu. Joseph Heco, too, had grown restless, writing, "Since the surveying ship was small, it rocked exceedingly, and I fell ill."[6] But he suffered from more than physical sickness. Child of a land-locked isolation, he was shaken anew by the immensity of the ocean. If the Americans were to linger over every little reef in the vast Pacific, he would never get home. There was a merchant ship in harbor bound for Hong Kong. Heco asked release from Brooke, and he was gone.

The *Cooper* had already taken on another Japanese, called variously Timoro, Timmors, and Tim, also the survivor of a shipwrecked junk. He had been rescued by an American ship aboard which he had chased whales for two years. When the *Cooper*'s men found him in Honolulu, he was consumed with homesickness. He had learned a little English, and Brooke, thinking he might be useful, signed him on board.

Before the *Cooper* left Hawaii, the American commissioner suggested a survey of Johnston Island, a rich guano

6. Hikozo, *Hyorya Ki: Floating on the Pacific Ocean* (Los Angeles, 1955), p. 60.

deposit on a half-mile islet to the southwest, which, he intimated, was in for some trouble. On March 14 the *Cooper*, taking the commissioner's advice, skirted the tails of reef that shoot like the fringe of a giant squid to the north of Johnston, and approached the low island by its quiet western lagoon. They were still outside the reef when a tiny boat sallied out to learn the *Cooper*'s intentions. Johnston Island, the *Cooper* learned, was already in a state of war, a war over guano, with one camp at the moment precariously holding the field in ominous quiet.[7]

A. D. Piper of the Pacific Guano Company, now in armed but watchful possession, had grandiose ideas for the island. He had had some experience in one of the earliest surveys of San Francisco; now for Johnston he planned railways and wharves, marked channels in the lagoon, even blasted some of the reef, and envisioned three hundred tons of guano a day, loaded at moderate expense. The company began to send commissioned ships. The *Harvey Birch* arrived in December, but discovered sunken rocks near its anchorage and refused to come near enough for the lighters to reach and unload her. In January the *Abby Brown* so badly injured herself in getting over the reef that she had to return unloaded to Honolulu for repairs.

The little *Cooper* had no authority to enter the war of competing guano claims, but her surveying instruments could legitimately chart the tangled corals. For three days, therefore, she worked over the islet and its lagoons, gave Piper copies of the findings, and then left the Pacific Guano Company to its own devices. While Lieutenant Thorburn had directed the soundings, Kern had spent most of his time on shore, sketching, stuffing birds, and preserving fish.[8]

Westward the schooner sailed along the fringes of Micronesia, chasing down shoals and islets like a bird pursuing

7. A. Piper to J. Brooke, March 17, 1859, Navy Branch, National Archives; printed in 36th Cong., 1st Sess., Sen. Ex. Doc. 2, pp. 1172–76.

8. Brooke, "Brooke," p. 635.

mackerel. On the charts they erased more fictitious rocks and relocated some which were so poorly placed "as to render the navigator liable to wreck, by the very course he pursues in endeavoring to avoid them."[9] They corrected designations, like two specks near Gaspar Rico (the modern Taongi northeast of Bikini) which were labeled Rabbit and Fruitful Islands, but which were found by Brooke and Kern to be, not islands, but only reefs of coral sand, surrounded by water "as blue as that of the deep sea." This careful analysis of the navigational hazards was probably the most important contribution of their voyage. Later, a reporter from the *Hong Kong Mail,* after an interview with Brooke, estimated that the *Cooper's* work had reduced by one-fifth the number of dangers in the California–China route.[10]

Guam, where they stayed three weeks, Brooke described as the only suitable harbor in the Marianas for a coal depot. The Spanish Governor, Don Felipe de la Corte, himself an engineer, took an active interest in the *Cooper's* work, particularly the astronomy and the rating of the chronometers. Hour after hour he talked with Brooke and Kern about harbor configuration, other islands in the group, morality, rights of foreigners, epidemics, earthquakes, and the cyclones which sometimes swept these southern Marianas.

On the evening of April 16 in Port Apra on Guam, Brooke was ashore, Lieutenant Thorburn was in charge of the ship, and Ned was on board. The barometer began falling steadily and a fresh wind brought squalls of rain. By midnight the barometer had fallen even lower, and the wind blew a gale. When the first anchor dragged, another was thrown overboard and backed by two kedges (lighter anchors). But to no avail. The wind, now a raging cyclone, dragged the *Cooper* relentlessly toward the harbor reef where the surf exploded in ragged sheets of spray. The

9. J. Brooke to I. Toucey, May 25, 1859, Navy Branch, National Archives.
10. As quoted in *National Intelligencer,* Sept. 9, 1859.

schooner was so wrapped in darkness and dripping winds that it was impossible to see from bow to stern. The deck boats went awash and Ned could hear them crashing in the breakers on the reef. He slogged about helping prepare to cut away the masts. Suddenly the night was filled with a single flash of lightning, the sickening smell of sulfur, and a blast of thunder. It was the vortex of the storm. The wind veered suddenly, and the *Cooper* swung clear of the reef.

No dramatist could have devised a more hairbreadth escape. When the storm abated, a schooner which had lain near the *Cooper* in the harbor was found on its beam ends, broken on the reef. Brooke, delighted to find his ship safe, though battered, at daybreak methodically recorded the cyclone and determined anew to find laws governing the paths of Pacific storms.

They were two weeks in Hong Kong and more weeks among the islands south of Japan, and on August 13, 1859, they sailed into the harbor of Kanagawa. Brooke distributed eight bottles of champagne to the crew for a celebration.

At the American consulate they met their recent shipmate, Joseph Heco, already official translator for the consul and a very happy young man. Through a fortunate meeting with Townsend Harris, first Consul General and Minister to Japan, Heco had been employed in the consulate at Kanagawa, and had even helped raise the American flag over a new consular building on July 4, 1859.

Kern found a different Japan from the one he had left four years before. The official world was torn between a distrust of and a desire to encourage the foreigner. The common people still were awed and fearful of the Americans, much as they had been as the launch "Vincennes Junior" touched the forbidden harbors in 1855, but now there was more open resentment. They were to see this animosity in the streets of Yokohama in the months ahead; yet even sooner they would find kindness and cooperation.

On August 16 Brooke left Thorburn in charge of the
ship and took Kern with him to Tokyo for talks with Townsend Harris. They traveled horseback, with hired attend-
ants, and enjoyed the food and the entertainment of "one
or two pretty girls" in the handsome inns along the way.
Harris had expected the *Cooper* and had plans for its work
in Japan. His most recent treaty with the Japanese had
provided that another port, Niigata, should be opened to
the Americans; but if Niigata should be found unsuitable
for American vessels, then, both governments concurring,
a substitute might be selected on the western coast of Japan.
Harris already doubted the suitability of Niigata and needed accurate information on alternative ports. Brooke agreed
to begin the work as soon as the typhoon season ended in
the spring.[11]

Brooke and Kern were detained in Tokyo by heavy rains
and winds strong enough to cause some concern for the
Cooper. Several days later when they finally got through to
the consul's house in Kanagawa, they were greeted with a
startling message from Thorburn: "We are on shore. I have
saved what I could. You had better come quickly."[12] By
the time the two had found a rowboat on the shore it was
dark and the rain was falling hard, but they pulled out to
the schooner and saw their ship, inert as death, with the
waters of a high tide pounding and splashing her tilted deck.
Back on shore they located the men in their temporary
quarters and heard a saddening story.

Just after daybreak on August 23, the barometer drop-
ping, Thorburn had forecast a severe storm, and soon the
Cooper's two anchors were slowly dragging in seas which
rolled so heavily that even in four fathoms her keel struck
the muddy bottom. The crew threw overboard all the
sounding shot and cannisters—anything to lighten the

11. Brooke, Journal, as quoted in Brooke, "Brooke," pp. 661–62.
12. Thorburn to Brooke, Aug. 22, 1859, as quoted in Brooke, "Brooke,"
p. 663.

thumping. By eight o'clock the winds and waves were wilder and the little *Cooper* was striking hard aft and dragging her anchors increasingly astern. The bows were pitching under mountainous waves. The thuddings unfooted the men and shattered the barometers. They were now in two fathoms. The carpenter yelled that the keel could not stand many more blows; she might already have opened below. Thorburn ordered a beaching.

By the slipping of one anchor, her bow was headed toward shore. The other anchor was buoyed, then cast off, and the gale rammed her onto the beach. She fell on her starboard side with the surf breaking.

The crew sloshed ashore, carrying instruments and record books wrapped in waterproofing. Thorburn saw that the hatches were secured, noted that the sea had entered below to the berth-deck beams, and finally left the ship.

A small group of Japanese had gathered on shore, curious and eager to aid in spite of the storm. They helped carry instruments and records to drier land. Local officials offered provisions and two houses for shelter. The buildings, one for the officers and one for the crew, were probably near the waterfront—at least they were in "the most dissolute part of the town."[13] But they were dry. Thorburn worked hard through the stormy afternoon getting the papers and surveying instruments under cover. Only a few instruments were broken or lost; all of the records were saved.

Inspection of the ship next day was disheartening. Brooke doubted that it could be ready for the sea even by spring. He wrote Harris canceling their plans for Niigata and admitted that the disappointment was "hard to bear." But there was still hope that the *Cooper* could be sailed again. Work began immediately with the crew ripping up planks to remove the ballast. Then, some days later when they reached the deepest layers in the viscera of the vessel, un-

13. J. Brooke to I. Toucey, Sept. 5, 1859, Navy Branch, National Archives.

damaged and never before inspected, they found at least forty of her skeletal timbers decayed almost through. Even the slim first hope had cracked.

None of the men, having seen the insides, wanted to sail her again, but Brooke thought it wise to seek outside corroboration. Most opportunely a Russian squadron of seven ships lay in Tokyo Bay to dignify a diplomatic mission under Count Muraviev-Amursky. The squadron's commander, Commodore A. A. Popoff, had already heard of the accident and given help in making early repairs. Brooke, knowing that Popoff had supervised the building of five ships for the Russian Navy, asked him to come down for professional consultation. Popoff with his squadron's carpenter crawled into the *Cooper's* hull and emerged with a decided opinion: take that rotten frame to sea, no matter how repaired superficially, and the ship would probably founder.[14]

They were stranded in Japan. Their ship, the *Cooper*, born the *Skiddy*, a New York harbor pilot-boat built of the old, whittled-down timbers of two clippers,[15] bought by Ringgold for the North Pacific Expedition and rechristened the *Cooper*, companion of the *Vincennes* to Japan, and surveyor of both Aleutian and South Pacific perils, was now sold to Japan and spent her last moldering days as a Japanese coastal tramp.

Meanwhile in the shore quarters, life proved full of incident. About eight-thirty in the evening of the third night on land two Dutch seamen burst into the house crying murder. Ned and Brooke ran with them for half a mile where they found in the street a dead Russian sailor, his skull crushed open. Beside him lay an officer, still conscious but in excruciating pain. Across his head were deep sabre cuts. Gashes over his shoulders and back exposed the joints and vertebrae, and across his thigh ran another agonizing

14. A. Popoff to J. Brooke, Sept. 9, 1859, Navy Branch, National Archives.
15. Brooke, Journal, Sept. 18, 1859, as quoted in Brooke, "Brooke," p. 671.

wound. Japanese police held off a small group of people, but none dared help or touch the Russian foreigners. Brooke did what he could and Ned raced back for the *Cooper*'s crew.

On a litter they carried the officer to a house near theirs. An American doctor came but gave no encouragement; all they could do, he said, was to ease the last hours. The man died at one o'clock in the morning.

In Yokohama and Tokyo the foreign community shuddered. Ned, perhaps through Heco, heard rumors that the Russians intended to burn Kanagawa, to attack Tokyo, to exact all manner of retribution. The Japanese officials expressed sorrow and regret, even attending the funeral though this action was proscribed by their religion.

No indemnity was asked, however. Count Muraviev, head of the Russian delegation, grandiloquently stated that Russia did not sell the blood of her subjects. He may have been aware that the murder reflected the widespread Japanese revulsion at foreign infiltration; and that to pursue the incident would be to aggravate the cause. As it was, the Russian murder was only the first of six assassinations of foreigners which occurred while Kern and Brooke were in Japan. And the foreigners were not alone; a far greater number of Japanese were mysteriously disappearing from offices or being found headless as a result of the widening rift between pro-foreign and anti-foreign political camps.[16]

To Brooke and Kern, Admiral Popoff brought warm personal thanks. Count Muraviev through diplomatic channels expressed his recognition of a "humane and friendly action," and Townsend Harris wrote from the United States Legation, "Spontaneous acts of this kind, do more to create and confirm a good understanding between Nations, than Scores of Diplomatic letters."[17]

16. Payson J. Treat, *Diplomatic Relations Between the United States and Japan: 1853–1895, I* (2 vols. Stanford, 1932), 94–96.
17. T. Harris to J. Brooke, Aug. 31, 1859; J. Brooke to I. Toucey, Sept. 5, 1859, Navy Branch, National Archives.

The house in which the Americans were quartered stood in a disreputable section of Kanagawa. Liquor, loose women, all sorts of temptations surrounded them; saki shops stood only a few steps from the door. Ned bunked with Brooke and Thorburn in a separate dwelling, but he was well aware of frequent drunkenness in the crew's quarters. On September 4 at about five o'clock in the afternoon, Thorburn came shouting, "A row among our men."

With the wave of murders on his mind, Brooke tucked two revolvers in his belt and followed. In the crew's house they found one man bleeding in a corner and the others in a circle around two drunks who were violently grappling amid broken furniture. Thorburn tried to separate them. Brooke drew a pistol. A shot followed. A seaman, Robert Weir, was struck in the right half of his chest; fifteen days later he died.

Though Brooke rationalized the whole incident into a moral on "the evil consequences which flow from insubordination,"[18] it lent itself more obviously to a moral on the consequences of long confining a ship's crew ashore. The Weir shooting was only one of a series of brawls and knifings and disratings. Not the least of the complications must have been Ned's epilepsy. By this time his attacks were occurring on an average of one every four or five months. To what extent they disabled him and for how long each time, we do not know. But apparently they did not seriously interfere with his work, for during these months he and Brooke, taking advantage of the available expedients and in spite of the confusions, engaged in a good deal of survey work on nearby coasts and harbors.[19]

Brooke was trying hard, though, to find passage home. The best hope was the U.S.S. *Powhatan,* expected sometime

18. J. Brooke to I. Toucey, Sept. 5, 1859, Navy Branch, National Archives.
19. The epilepsy reference is from John Brooke, Journal, as quoted in letter from George M. Brooke, Jr., to R. V. Hine, March 20, 1960. Brooke, "Brooke," pp. 686–87.

in September to transport the first Japanese ambassadors to the United States. The *Powhatan,* however, did not arrive until November, two months later, and by then the diplomatic negotiations had snarled. The treaty which Townsend Harris concluded with the shogunate in 1858 had stipulated final ratification ceremonies in Washington, D.C. For that purpose the Japanese delegation had prepared to board the *Powhatan.* But those Japanese who loathed the foreigners and were using their presence as a political weapon against the shogunate, now vehemently insisted that such an embassy would flout Japanese laws against travel abroad. More delays. In January of the new year, 1860, although the *Powhatan* temporarily returned to Hong Kong, political carping was apparently subsiding and plans for the voyage progressed even to near completion. On the *Powhatan's* return in February, after nearly six months of waiting, it looked as if Brooke and Kern and the others would soon steam homeward.[20]

The pro-foreign element in the shogunate had meanwhile decided to extend itself, not only to send the ambassadors aboard the *Powhatan,* but also to dispatch to California Japan's first warship. As an indication of its enlarging foreign interests, the shogunate in 1857 had bought a Dutch, ten-gun, bark-rigged screw steamer, and named it the *Kanrin Maru.* It would now be the first craft of a fledgling Japanese Navy to cross the Pacific.

She was to carry some of the best Japanese naval and engineering minds available—Admiral Kimura, Settsu-no-kami, Captain Katsu Rintaro (later Count Katsu Awa, the first Navy Minister of the Meiji government), and the American-trained Nakahama Manjiro—but the shogunate hoped to safeguard the ship and also expand limited Japanese

20. Allan B. Cole, "Japan's First Embassy to the United States, 1860," *Pacific Northwest Quarterly, 32* (1941), 131–66; Chitoshi Yanaga, "The First Japanese Embassy to the United States," *Pacific Historical Review, 9* (1940), 113–38.

navigational knowledge by requesting a few American officers to travel on the *Kanrin Maru* as advisers. When Brooke
heard of the proposal, he volunteered and asked that Ned
Kern be allowed to accompany him. Ten other members
of the *Cooper* crew were also accepted for the voyage on
this first official Japanese vessel to visit the United States.
Thorburn and the remaining men of the *Cooper* sailed on
the *Powhatan* a few days later.

The *Kanrin Maru* left Uragawa harbor on February 10,
1860, with its complement of fifty-seven Japanese plus the
group from the ill-fated *Cooper*. Ned and Brooke were assigned the choice after-cabins, sumptuous with polished ma-
hogany, and received every attention, including the services
of a staff of servants.

The day of departure Captain Katsu took sick and was
confined to his room for almost the entire trip. Rough
weather set in straightway, and Brooke and Kern soon observed that the voyage was not to be a normal one by American Navy standards. Even in scudding winds and high seas,
no more than two or three of the crew were on deck. During
the first weeks the officers did not even keep watch, or did
so only intermittently and as the spirit moved them—and
this on a ship over three times the size of the *Cooper*.
Brooke's systematic nature was aroused, and he probably
expressed his views openly; at any rate, he reported later
that "the Japanese improved as they acquired experience."[21]

The improvement probably resulted as much from American example as from American advice. The Japanese crew
had never sailed the high seas—they had taken their ship
on short coastal cruises between Nagasaki and Tokyo, but
mostly through the Inland Sea and under steam. Now in
their straw sandals they were asked to furl topsails in gale
weather and they either did not know what to do or were

21. J. Brooke to I. Toucey, March 20, 1860, Navy Branch, National Archives.

terrified of doing it. They accidentally broke in the sky-lights; they set fire to the galley; and when Ned investigated a large Japanese box which was banging about the cabin, the Americans were startled and appalled to find it filled with about forty thousand percussion caps. The *Cooper's* crew meanwhile clambered into the rigging, righted the sails, and instructed the Japanese. Brooke and Kern helped navigate and set the course.[22]

Not all of the Japanese, however, were novice seamen, and they were proud of their burgeoning navigational knowledge. Brooke admitted that the engineers were com-petent and that some of the officers made skilled astronom-ical observations. One of their most able men was Naka-hama Manjiro, who, like Joseph Heco, had as a boy been rescued as a castaway, educated in New England, had stud-ied navigation on a Yankee whaler, and returned to Japan to translate Bowditch's *Navigator* and even play a behind-the-scenes part in the Perry negotiations. He now sailed the *Kanrin Maru* as navigator and interpreter. Brooke called him a "fine fellow indeed," and was convinced that his in-telligence "had more to do with the opening of Japan than any other man living."[23]

The Americans were glad to teach; the Japanese were eager to learn. The weather may have been rough, but only "the most perfect harmony," to use Brooke's words, existed between the races.

22. Brooke, Journal, Feb. 15, 1860, as quoted in Brooke, "Brooke," p. 708. Yukichi Fukuzawa, personal servant of the Admiral on this voyage, claimed in his *Autobiography* (Tokyo, 1948), pp. 118–19, that the Japanese had no help from the Americans whatsoever, but his chapter is so clearly geared to presenting the Japanese in the best light that Brooke's report to the Secretary of the Navy on the subject seems more reliable. See also the diary of Muragaki Awaji-no-kami in American–Japan Society, *The First Japanese Embassy to the United States* (Tokyo, 1920), p. 19, which supports Brooke, as does also a report from Brooke in the Hydrographic Office File No. 271.1, Navy Branch, National Archives.

23. Brooke, "Brooke," pp. 702, 705, both quoting from Brooke, Journal.

On March 17, 1860, thirty-seven days out of Japan, Ned stood under a Japanese flag watching the Golden Gate emerge from the Berkeley Hills, and finally saw the Bay fling its arms to north and south. A red-ball flag on a Japanese ship in San Francisco Bay! For the first time in history! Reporters from the *Alta California* were aboard before the docking at Vallejo Street. They toured the ship, noted its polished cleanliness, and centered their questions on Brooke and Kern. The next day's papers were full of the details of the trip which the two had given them.

Commercial circles saw the *Kanrin Maru* as a precursor of a whole new era of Pacific trade, with ships steaming regularly between Tokyo and San Francisco. The newspapers said the *Kanrin Maru* was pioneering abroad "to break up the exclusiveness of centuries," and that its presence pointed up once more the national obligation to construct a transcontinental railroad to San Francisco. A lead editorial noted the loss of the *Cooper* and called for other ships to finish its job.[24]

Ned helped Brooke show the town to the Japanese. The visitors wanted to know American bathing customs, so they all immersed themselves at the San Francisco Baths on Washington Street. (Ned may have made veiled references to the more civilized practice of separating the sexes in public bathing.) They watched iron being cast at the Vulcan factory; they toured the gas works and were offered champagne among the machinery. They inspected the government mint, shipyards, and sugar refineries. Everywhere crowds surrounded their carriages.

On the fourth day Admiral Kimura, his officers, Brooke, and Kern came ashore for the official reception. At Job's Hotel, after meats, chicken salads, custards, and creams, rounds of champagne toasts began. Two cultures saluted

24. *Weekly Alta California,* March 24, 31, 1860.

one another, or as one newspaper said, "Punctilio and Dontcareism are 'taking a drink' together."[25]

The first toast was raised "To the Emperor of Japan and the President of the United States": three cheers standing. Admiral Kimura, wearing wide trousers with blue and gold spangles and white sandals, responded with the same toast, but diplomatically in reverse order. Manjiro translated. Corks popped and champagne flowed. Toasts followed to Admiral Kimura, to the American Army and Navy, to the Governor of California, to the Pacific Railroad—"the greatest project of the age"—and to John Brooke.

The final toast was to Edward Kern. Frederick MacCrellish, editor of the *Alta California* proposed it, and John Brooke added a tribute to his friend. As the glasses were raised and the cheers sounded, Ned, though usually not sentimental, must have been moved by this sparkling recognition. At the end of a year and a half of taking soundings and making surveys, hunting guano rocks and submerged reefs, fighting high seas and cyclone winds, a period which might represent the furthest extension of his science and the widest applications of his art, he had returned to San Francisco to be toasted in champagne.

25. *Frank Leslie's Illustrated Newspaper,* May 26, 1860, referring to a later celebration.

CHAPTER 7

St. Louis and Philadelphia

The summer of 1860 brought Ned home again, but as with all previous expeditions the tedious job of digesting the field notes had only begun. It was the year of Lincoln's election, and Ned, helping Brooke at the Naval Observatory in Washington, could hardly avoid debating with his southern friend the fate of the Union. Brooke, bending over the drawing boards, was reserved, but he was as determined as his pen was meticulous. He had always defended slavery on the grounds that the Negroes were an inferior race. Industrial societies like the North and England, he was convinced, treated their workingmen far worse than the South its slaves; the Abolitionists simply did not know what they were talking about; and it might even be a good thing to reopen the African slave trade. After Lincoln's inauguration and the fall of Fort Sumter, on the same day Robert E. Lee and Matthew Fontaine Maury resigned from their services, Brooke withdrew from the United States Navy to serve Virginia. "When the state of Virginia seceded, in accordance with my convictions, I laid down my pencil on the chart of

'French Frigate Shoals' which I was drawing, went to the
Navy Department and handed in my resignation."[1]

Without Brooke and in the confusion of the first days
of war, the expedition's tabulations were pushed into a
closet. The little *Cooper* had been a casualty of a typhoon;
the processing of its findings became a casualty of war.

Contrary to his usual impetuosity, Ned waited to enlist
for war duty. The great national convulsion did not immediately appeal to this particular man of curiosity; perhaps
because of his epilepsy he did not consider himself a good
military risk. Furthermore, when a nation falls apart, what
happens to the artist or the scientist? Where is his place in
the armed forces? Kern's topographical skills, his mathematical and astronomical abilities, even his scientific interests would seem to imply engineering, and in this case logic
proved itself. In July, after three months of waiting, Edward
was commissioned a Captain of Topographical Engineers.

In this there was nothing remarkable, but more surpris-
ing is the fact that Ned enlisted under John C. Frémont.
Kern was one of the new major general's first appointments,
effective only a matter of days after Frémont arrived in
Washington to assume command of the Army of the West.
Thus in the midst of civil war Ned rallied to the one-time
source of his bitterness. But why?

The motivations are not clear, though his hatred of Frémont obviously must have abated. Perhaps Dick before his
death had been a principal cause of the change. In 1851 on
his return from the Sitgreaves Expedition, Dick had for
some reason contacted Frémont in San Francisco, and the
two had evidently reached an understanding. All we actually know of this rapprochement is through Simpson, in one

1. J. Brooke to L. Brooke, June 12, 1859; J. Brooke to T. Jenkins, Sept.
15, 1881; as quoted in Brooke, "Brooke," pp. 646, 744. J. Snyder, in a letter
to E. Kern, Nov. 3, 1860, Fort Sutter Papers, suggested at this time that
Ned retire to California: "Just think of Old Kern under his own vine and
fig tree in the evening of his days."

of his moralistic letters to Dick: "I am glad you and Frémont have become reconciled to each other. There can be no doubt but he has done great injustice to individuals in his public career, but the first step toward improvement is to confess error, and as he seems to have done this in your case, there is hope that his experience will not be lost upon him."[2] The argument, whatever its foundation, might have influenced Ned when Dick returned.

Furthermore, the Army of the West was a congenial appointment. He had been promised a place on Frémont's own staff, unassigned to any company. Many of his California friends were reported flocking to their old commander, and Ned knew that John Pope was there as a brigadier general; ironically he and Pope now would both serve under the man they had once declared incompetent. Indeed, it was in St. Louis itself, their new headquarters, that Kern and Pope in 1851 had damned Frémont's mapping. Now St. Louis offered Ned a recall to the West, to the scenes of his happiest years and his most tragic memories.

He arrived in late July or early August, to find Confederate flags flying and secessionists rampant. Ned remembered the city as the bustling place whose wharves he had first seen on a spring day in 1845; but now the confusion covered a desperate local struggle. The military situation in Missouri was based, as Frémont said, on "A rebel faction in every county, at least equal to the loyal population in numbers, and excelling it in vindictiveness and energy."[3] But the men, in Mark Twain's words, were still in process of being turned "from rabbits to soldiers." As a matter of fact, young Sam Clemens marched at this very time with

2. J. Simpson to R. Kern, May 11, 1852, Huntington Library. It is true that in the 1856 presidential campaign Kern charges of Frémont's reprehensibility were gleefully quoted by the anti-Frémont stumpers, but it is possible that none of the statements were made by Ned after Dick's conversion in 1851.

3. John C. Frémont testimony, in U.S. Congress, *Report of the Joint Committee on the Conduct of the War, 3* (3 vols. Washington, 1863), 34.

southern forces. Confederates under Sterling Price and Benjamin McCulloch wandered almost at will over the state, inflicting serious defeats on the Union armies under Nathaniel Lyon. Clearly one of Frémont's first jobs was to assess the positions and potentials of the enemy. He needed scouts for spies, and Ned Kern was one of his first. Ned worked secretly under the direct command of the general. During August he made sweeping reconnaissance with Captain Charles de Arnaud, a French engineer who had served in the Crimean War. They ranged close to Confederate lines—dangerous business in Tennessee and Kentucky near the fires of Polk and Pillow—and returned with sketches of roads, pikes, railroads, enemy camps, and masked batteries.[4] It was this work which paved the way for Grant's move on Paducah.

The mission with de Arnaud suggests a picture of Ned's days in Missouri. He was part of a highly cosmopolitan staff, drawn not only from the Mississippi Valley and the Far West, but more noticeably from western Europe. Kern must have spun countless tales of western expeditions to Europeans who, like de Arnaud, bore foreign names and spoke with foreign accents: Cattanco and Saccippi and Occidone, Asboth and Fiala and Zagonyi.[5] The West had always held fascination for Europeans, and here was Ned with Frémont's other western veterans working over maps in the basement of the Brant house or congregating before field kitchens, making a point with a sketch on a scrap of paper, retelling the stories of grizzly, of rattler, of Navajo, of señorita—the still fresh legends of the West.

In October 1861 Ned marched southwest with the Army on the drive to liberate Springfield, to quiet guerrilla warfare, and perhaps to trap Price's Confederates. Frémont

4. E. Kern to Frémont, Aug. 11, 1861, Old Army Branch, National Archives.

5. Francis Grierson, *Valley of Shadows* (Boston, 1909), p. 234; Nevins, *Frémont* (1939), pp. 476, 494.

labored under heavy criticism from conservatives for his August emancipation proclamation. His vociferous Missouri enemies, the Blairs, charged him with extravagance, tyranny, and neglect of duty. As Allan Nevins puts it, "Working night and day under a sword of Damocles, he knew that within a few weeks the thread which sustained it would probably break."[6] The Secretary of War had even shown Frémont an order for his dismissal waiting to be served. For Frémont Springfield was not only the key to the area; it was the hinge of his own fate in Missouri.

On the way, near Warsaw, Ned helped bridge the Osage River which lay like a cordon before the Army. Here the engineers built in thirty-six hours a span eight hundred feet long, sawing their own green lumber. An eyewitness described Kern with the others "down on the bank, directing the busy workmen, and shaping the rough hewn trestles, measuring and cutting stringer and brace, fixing rope and chain and bolt, and putting through the more important preparatory work."[7]

No one could have been better prepared in the skillful devising of expedients. No hiker of a western trail knew better the kinds of trees to cut, the spot on a river best to bridge. The years in New Mexico of drawing on whatever paper was at hand, the months on Japanese or Siberian shores improvising barometer tubes or presses in which to dry camellias, these were the experiences which now helped to build an eight-hundred-foot bridge in thirty-six hours.

"The fall rains were over; the fine weather of the Indian summer had come; the hay was gathered and corn hardening, and we were about to carry out the great object of our campaign, under the most favorable auspices, with fewer hardships from exposure, and impediments from transpor-

6. Nevins, *Frémont* (1939), p. 529.

7. A letter from "H," Oct. 19, 1861; as quoted in Jessie Frémont, *The Story of the Guard* (Boston, 1863), p. 98. See also Nevins, *Frémont* (1939), p. 533.

tation, than at any other season."[8] So Frémont later testi-
fied. But though Indian summer came and went, the battle
of Springfield was never fought. Instead, Ned witnessed
the thoroughgoing despondency, the throwing down of carbines, the threats of mutiny which the news of Frémont's
recall produced in the Army. For all his impulsiveness and
bullheadedness, Frémont was a man to stir deep loyalties,
and Ned Kern, who had marched at his side and sat at his
feet, who had for a time hated his name only to return at
last to his fealty, was embodied proof of the magnetism.

Soon after the recall of the general on November 2, 1861,
Ned's commission was revoked. It, like Frémont's other
commissions, had been irregular, with no official enrolling
by the Adjutant General; hence the Army said there could
be no pay.[9] Meanwhile Ned went back to Philadelphia having nothing to show for his service in Missouri, just as he
had had nothing to show for his work with Frémont in
1848–49. Perhaps that is why he did not volunteer again.
He set up a studio on Chestnut Street—for the third time
in his life trying to pick up as a teacher of drawing, where
he had left off in 1845.

Through 1862 and into the summer and fall of 1863 the
war news in the Philadelphia papers swirled Ned backward
in time. Joseph Revere, who once helped Ned crush the
"spider" Walla Wallas, now was being court-martialed on
charges of retreating without orders at Chancellorsville.
James Simpson had survived a Confederate prison, been
exchanged, and wore the bars of colonel in the Fourth New
Jersey Volunteers. John Parke as a major general had served
as Burnside's chief-of-staff at Antietam and in June of 1863

8. U.S. Congress, *Report of the Joint Committee*, 3, 43.
9. Eventual recompense came through a special bill in Congress; *Cong.
Globe*, 37th Cong., 2nd Sess., pp. 1280–81. Edward had similar troubles with
his bounty land warrants and a bonus payment for the North Pacific Exploring Expedition; see memorial "To the Honorable Senate and House
of Reps. . . ." (n.d.), Box 131, Naval Foundation Papers, Library of Congress.

was holding the extreme right flank of Grant's siege at Vicksburg. John Pope, after his days in Missouri, meteorically rose to command the Army of Virginia and then lost grace before Lee and Jackson at the Second Battle of Manassas.

Of his naval companions, John Brooke, friend of his sea days, though a rebel to his flag, had appropriately found a berth as chief of the Confederate Bureau of Ordnance and Hydrography. John Rodgers, on the other hand, regilded for the Union the naval fame of his family. For a few weeks in September of 1861 he had hoped to manage Frémont's gunboats on the Mississippi, and Ned may have seen him in St. Louis during those turbulent days. A commodore, Rodgers had more recently headed the line in an attack on Fort Sumter. And the *Vincennes,* which for three of Ned's years had been a home, from the dripping doldrums of Hong Kong to the storms off Siberia, now captured British coffee ships and took Confederate prizes in the Gulf of Mexico. So the war, as periods of crisis often do, exposed to Ned Kern the men and the threads which once tangled with his own life, and he could sit like Clio reviewing a life's history, while he read the papers and waited for students.

These two years were uneventful for Ned. His name and experience would have attracted some pupils, but it is hard to imagine that in the midst of civil war the demand for drawing instruction would have been great.

The teacher's heart, moreover, could hardly have been in his work. He was still young, not yet forty. His temperament was not so changed that he would have been ready to settle down, to anchor himself permanently. Over what future vistas his mind might have run! With what colors he might have sketched the next exploration, and the one after that!

But Ned Kern had traveled his final westward expedition. The quietness of his last days was a notable contrast to those of Ben and Dick. Ned, the initiator of the wanderings

of the Kerns, the one of the three who had been longest in
the field and subject to the greatest dangers, died in bed at
home in Philadelphia on November 23, 1863. It was the
Thanksgiving season, the time when cottonwoods turned at
Westport, when the Sacramento River ran low, when snow
fell in the San Juans, when heavy rains poured on the Japanese coast. His death certificate attributed the cause to
epileptic convulsions. The funeral was held at the home of
his brother John.[10] Might John, "the old man," reminded
by the sprays of funeral flowers, have recalled the larkspur
seeds he sent to Santa Fe fourteen years before? Then he had
sought to dispel the gloom of Ned and Dick who were
mourning the death of Ben. Now all three of them, his
younger brothers, were gone.

> Long having wander'd since, round the
>   earth having wander'd
> Now I face home again . . .

And might John, too, have pondered the perverse nature
of the Kern fortune? Ned's life, for example, had been full
enough, fuller than his forty years would suggest, but it
was also characterized by recurrent adversities, each of
which veiled his work from all but those immediately concerned. The Frémont third expedition on which Ned enjoyed his first successes as artist, as topographer, and even
as commander at Fort Sutter, was, unlike Frémont's earlier
expeditions, never reported. No handsome quarto, printed
by the thousands at government expense and illustrated,
as it would have been, with Edward Kern's lithographs,
glorified the third expedition. Instead the unsavory blus-
terings and vituperations of the 1847 court-martial lingered
in the public mind as the ignominious end of the tour
which began so auspiciously. The Frémont fourth expedi-

10. He was buried in Glenwood Cemetery and later moved to New
Glenwood Cemetery. For funeral notice, see Philadelphia *Ledger*, Nov. 28,
1863.

tion, which left a third of its members dead of starvation and cold, certainly produced no public acclaim for anyone, let alone Ned. The reports of the North Pacific Exploring Expedition were never printed intact, in contrast to those of the Wilkes Expedition which only a few years before had resulted in six magnificent volumes rich with lithographs and engravings. The North Pacific findings, largely because of the bickerings of commanders over credits for a larger publication, were only slowly absorbed into the comparative obscurity of scientific journals. And the Brooke survey was doomed by a Japanese typhoon and a civil war.

Symbolic of Ned's apparent fate to remain unrecognized and somewhat anonymous is a comparatively insignificant event which occurred during his days in New Mexico. The census of 1850 did not mention Edward Kern as living anywhere in that territory. Although he had resided there for over a year and although his brother was working in the census office, at the time of the actual count Ned was on the road, having left Abiquiu before the lists were taken, and he arrived in Santa Fe just after they were finished. At both ends he missed the roll.

Even when Ned enjoyed successes, they were inexorably followed by frustrations. The third expedition, which included the excitement and responsibility of Fort Sutter, led to the lacerations of the fourth, when Ned lost not only a brother and gold but respect for his commander as well. The North Pacific Expedition, though unpublicized, still held for Ned the personal satisfaction of finishing his maps and drawings; but it was followed by his work with Brooke, which was destined to be curtailed by the typhoon. The final disappointment (and this one had little of success to precede it) was his service with Frémont during the Civil War. His irregular commission excluded him even from a listing in the official records, and his assignments were often secret. Only by surviving the duration of the war, which he did not do, could he have adequately petitioned for recognition;

and nothing that we know of his character leads to the belief that he would have so petitioned. Ned's consistent deprivation of fame and fortune may have prompted his comment on the losses of 1849 as being typical of "family luck."

But, despite the misfortunes, there was much of fulfillment. Edward Kern lived, as his obituary said, a "varied and industrious" life. The variety was a result of his having been a scientist as well as an artist. Newspapers referred to him (and his brother Richard) sometimes as the one, sometimes as the other, seldom mentioning the two fields together. But for the Kerns the two dovetailed beautifully, and they would want to be remembered as both.

As scientists they lived at a time in world history when the great geographical discoveries were largely accomplished but the careful surveying of the earth's surface had only begun. It was the day of the topographer, and in this work the Kerns shone clearly. Mapmaking was sure of a result, "sure as the stars which had their part in it," as Frémont said;[11] it called for qualities of exactness and accuracy, which were notable in the Kerns.

Ned learned topography largely from Frémont, and hence he carried on the French civil-engineering tradition brought to this country by Nicollet and Hassler, Frémont's teachers. Kern's work with telescope and barometer paved the way for Preuss' map accompanying Frémont's *Geographical Memoir*. He helped draft the projection for Simpson's 1849 report on the Navajo expedition. He translated on paper much of Pope's reconnaissance from Santa Fe to Fort Leavenworth. And the wall-size charts of the Ringgold–Rodgers expedition abound with Kern's sketches of coast and headland, often carefully identified with surveyor's angles. It is interesting, too, that one of the few bits of evidence of Ned's Civil War service and the last known docu-

11. As quoted in John C. Frémont, *Narratives of Exploration and Adventure* ed., Allan Nevins (New York, 1956), p. 75.

ment in his hand is a small field map, covered with the notes of latitude and longitude, triangulation, and distance that characterized so much of his life's activity.[12] *(Fig. 53)*

The Kerns also made serious efforts to amass data for the embryonic study of ethnology. Their interest was, of course, stimulated by Frémont's concern with native peoples and the important contributions to the field already made by men like Bodmer and Catlin, and it went beyond common curiosity and culminated in efforts to understand the economies and cultures of various western Indian communities. Ned's ethnological pursuits, which began on the trail in 1845, flowered in California where his position at Fort Sutter brought him into contact with Hokan and Penutian tribes. His observation of their crafts and rituals later provided Schoolcraft with rare detail.

In New Mexico the Kerns filled their diaries with long descriptions of costumes, customs, and religious rites. Their drawings included studies of housing, sacred dances, weaving, even the colored patterns on pottery shards. Simpson in his report used Richard Kern's list of the Indian names for each of the chief pueblos, and he included Edward Kern's collection of a set of comparative words from the pueblos of San Juan, Santa Clara, San Ildefonso, Pojoaque, Nambe, and Tesuque.[13] When Simpson concluded, in opposition to some current opinion, that the Apache language was unrelated to that of the Pueblos, he should have credited the Kerns with help in reaching the conclusion.

Ned once advised Dick that the best preparation for the artist of a western expedition was the study of natural history. It was shrewd advice—at least three-fourths of the Kerns' productive time in the West was devoted to such an end. Without some knowledge of botany they could not

12. "Kern's Reconnaissance Notes from Rolla, Mo., westward to the Gasconade, 1861," Cartographic Branch, National Archives.
13. Gregg, *Commerce of the Prairies*, p. 187, used a similar grouping; and such lists of words were commonly found in western reports, e.g., Catlin, *Letters and Notes*, 2, Appendix.

have drawn plates of flowers and trees which would have any value for eastern scientists; without zoology, they could not have intelligently sketched creatures from mice to bison; without geology, their illustrations of mountains and passes would have been meaningless except as decorations. In all of these areas the Kerns produced beautiful examples of scientific drawing, carefully executed and arranged.

If a separate naturalist were included in the expedition, as Creutzfeldt had been on the Pacific Railroad survey or Stimpson on the North Pacific cruise, the Kerns were obligated to draw the lizards or flowers which the naturalist gave them; but frequently the choice of items to be sketched devolved on the artists themselves. As members of the Philadelphia Academy of Natural Sciences, they were not unprepared, and it is easy to imagine long sessions before each expedition in the Academy's library with their confreres briefing them on clues to coal strata, skeletal arrangement, or the details of a stamen.

Of course, the scientists in the East would prefer an actual specimen, instead of a drawing, if it could be carried; hence the Kern packs usually bulged with cans of limp lizards in brown alcohol, or dry stuffed birds. Skill in taxidermy was important, but even more important was a knowledge of what to collect. Here again, in order to be of real assistance to men like Leidy and Morton, the Kerns must themselves have training and exhibit judgment. The Smithsonian Institution welcomed their birds; scientific publications credited Edward with discovering varieties, such as two rare crustacea, and each time the Kerns returned to Philadelphia the Academy received from them new batches of beetles, grasshoppers, scorpions, moths, rodents, shells, or the bones of prairie wolves.[14] Since the days when

14. William Stimpson, "Report on the Crustacea Collected by the North Pacific Exploring Expedition," *Miscellaneous Collections of the Smithsonian Institution, 49* (Washington, 1907), 124, 127. Academy of Natural Sciences of Philadelphia, *Proceedings, 3* (1846–47), 213, 255; *4* (1848–49), 245; *5* (1850–51), 297; *6* (1852–53), vii, viii, xxvii; *12* (1860), donations of July 3.

Lewis and Clark sent back their crates to Jefferson, such collections had been typical results of expeditions in the Far West.

However considerable their contributions to various fields of science, and however much those contributions depended on their drawings, the Kerns were not first-rate artists. On artistic grounds their best work was sometimes as good as Catlin's and frequently compared well with that of Alfred Jacob Miller. But they never approached the emotional content and evocative insights of Carl Bodmer as he portrayed, for example, the elementary savagery of the Buffalo Dance. Bodmer was trained in Europe and in the best schools, but this is not the point. He possessed an imaginative flair which the Kerns never achieved, and although imagination is not the sole criterion of art, it is important. The Kerns were content to limn their Indians in flat profile or puppet-like activity. No Kern drawing approaches the intensity of Bodmer's portrait of Pehriska-Ruhpa gritting his teeth through his dog-dance feathers.

Artistically the best Kern works are probably Ned's Oriental sketches. They were products of his more mature years, and in them he achieved a freedom and skill beyond anything he or Dick had done in California or New Mexico. But even in the best of these, such as *Cutting up the Whale (Fig. 48)* or *Market at Napa (Fig. 44)* he lacks the verve of that witty Irish transplant to the Orient, George Chinnery, who a few years earlier was drawing similar subjects.

Nevertheless, Ned, if not Dick, is still remembered in the art galleries of this country. His water colors and oils are now owned by the Boston Museum of Fine Arts, the National Collection of Fine Arts in Washington, the Gilcrease Institute in Tulsa, and the Museum of the Naval Academy at Annapolis. One of the Naval Academy oils was chosen by the Corcoran Gallery to hang in its "American Processional" exhibition of 1950.

The Kerns flourished in an age of artistic Romanticism—

that special affirmation of the emotions, of the particular over the general, of the exotic in time and place. Thomas Cole and Thomas Doughty, Thomas Birch and Jasper Cropsey—these were among the Romantic painters whose works the Kerns absorbed during their youth. Well they knew the Hudson River School of landscape with its moody evocations, and the wind from the American West (was it Shelley's wild west wind?) blew in the same intellectual direction. A later group of Romantics, like Albert Bierstadt, substituted the Rocky Mountains for the Hudson River; the scene changed but not the technique and the moods. The West was attractive to Romantics, for one reason, because it was little enough known to be subject to legend. The trans-Mississippi West, like the fountains of Bimini or the pearls of Calafia, was still the stuff of dreams. In the Kerns' day the myth of the Great American Desert was being supplanted by the myth of the Garden of the West, while the myth of the Noble Savage continued its traditional clash with the myth of the Villainous Indian. But all were myths and all were Romantic; they were emotions and wishful thinking, not rational judgments of fact.

To what extent did the Kerns as topographic artists Romanticize their image of the West?

In this connection the important thing to remember about men like the Kerns is that their purposes were scientific and reportorial. Simpson or Sitgreaves or Gunnison, who hired them, did so because, as Frémont said, they could "hold these lovely views in all their delicate coloring,"[15] that is, capture the scene exactly. The proposal to include a camera lucida, a shadow box to help the artist accurately reproduce the subject, as part of Kern's equipment on the third expedition suggests the artistic goal, as does Ned's later experimentation with photography. It might be noted that Eugene Delacroix, the French painter,

15. Frémont, *Memoirs*, p. 486.

was employed about the same time to illustrate a diplomatic mission to Algiers. His resulting "documents," however, were highly Romantic, imaginative interpretations of an exotic land. The Kerns, even if they had had the skill of Delacroix, had as scientists been trained to avoid Romanticization.

They themselves held few illusions about the West. They were intensely curious, but their natural reactions tended to be skeptical with a liberal laugh for the overblown. Nothing in any of their writings remotely approaches Catlin's description of Indians "whose daily feats, with their naked limbs, might vie with those of the Grecian youths in the beautiful rivalry of the Olympian games."[16] On the contrary, the Kerns not only depicted some Indian women as "up and down like a plank board,"[17] but found whole tribes, like the Mojaves, ugly, dirty, and villainous. They did evaluate Cheyenne art work or Pomo crafts with real appreciation, but never did they see the West in terms of idealized Indians surrounded by an exotic land.

Yet judging from the lithographs taken from Kern sketches, the brothers seem frequently to stylize and exaggerate for effect, rather like F. W. Egloffstein who followed them into the Southwest. Dick's tall, balloon-like version of the cliffs above Casa Blanca in Canyon de Chelly *(Fig. 26)* are as fantastic as were Egloffstein's engravings of brooding Grand Canyon spires. The Kerns might seem, therefore, to have succumbed in the field to Romantic influences.

But not necessarily so. One of the curious things about the Kerns' work is that few of these Romantic touches are present in the original sketches and drawings; they appear rather in the subsequent lithographs and engravings. The transition here from sketch to lithograph is important. Few western artists made their own lithographic stones, although Edward did at one time advise Dick to learn the

16. Catlin, *Letters and Notes, 1,* 15.
17. E. Kern to R. Kern, June 1845, Fort Sutter Papers.

technique. In most cases an eastern firm like Duvals of Philadelphia or Sarony of New York would draw on the limestone, presumably in the process following the sketches as closely as possible. The 1840's and the 1850's were the golden age of lithography and each lithographic house catered to a wide public. This meant, for one thing, that the lithographers tended to develop their own individual styles which became almost unconsciously superimposed on the work of the artists.[18] It also meant that when certain details had to be supplied to a sketchy drawing, the lithographer was apt to depict his own concepts or those which he felt would please his clientele. Thus when Ackerman in New York rendered Dick's sketch of a New Mexico blacksmith shop, he completely changed the perspective, vastly enlarged the room, and clothed the Indians like European medieval artisans.

In the final analysis, the artistic accomplishment of Ned Kern, like the perverse nature of his fortune, tended to be distorted. His drawing, his image of the West, was to be seen in large part through the dark glass of a lithographer.

This fact was true of the artists of most of the early government reports—of Frémont, of Simpson, of Sitgreaves, of Emory—and it may help explain why the Romantic image of the West so long persisted. Again and again the West was to appear as a garden of valleys with gossamer clouds behind craggy peaks. The desert, given water, would bloom, and the denuded hills would conceal all kinds of color and mystery. The topographic artists often did not see it that way; they were more apt to be scientific in their orientations. But partly because of their lithographers, their voices might as well have been raised to stop that wild west wind from trumpeting its prophecy.

The lives of the Kerns, Romantic by temperament, scientific by training, coincided remarkably with the key areas

18. Harry T. Peters, *America on Stone* (Garden City, New York, 1931), p. 31.

of their nation's explosive expansion. Where there were frontiers of acquisition, exploration, or commercial expansion, there was Richard for five years and Edward for fifteen. Ned, like his brother, might not have understood the economic and political forces behind manifest destiny, but he reflected mightily a kindred drive, a volunteering spirit to leave the trail, a fever to sleep on unexplored ground, whether on the shores of the Great Salt Lake or the Sagami Sea. Like the America of his day, he was not meant to stay home, to teach, quietly to conserve. His destiny, like America's, was to move, to expand, to touch horizons, to feel consuming curiosity. As Byron said, "Motion was in their days." And the call came to Edward Kern, a sensitive, artistic intellect who on the basis of his background ought logically to have found more congenial the centers of culture and comfort; but on these he turned his back time and time again. This restlessness was his daemon. It drove him from struggle to struggle, from misfortune to misfortune, to ice storms and the presence of death, to heat and the presence of insanity, to typhoons, shipwrecks, and the loss of two brothers. Yet he no more could have denied this daemon than could John Charles Frémont or Jedediah Smith or the Ohio farmer who pulled stakes when he heard the far sound of an axe in the still morning, no more than the sap can stay in the roots when the spring winds blow.

Bibliographical Essay

The Kerns and the West

Primary

The most extensive collection of Kern letters and journals is in the Huntington Library. The original Fort Sutter Papers (which are in effect Edward Kern Papers) are there, though transcripts of these are also available in a few other key libraries across the country. They include 161 items, mostly letters, jottings, and official reports, 119 of which are in the period from 1845 to 1847. All but five of the papers were written before 1854, and even the subsequent five throw little light on Kern's experience in the Pacific.

Also in the Huntington Library is a series of diaries kept by the Kern brothers from 1848 to 1851, the New Mexico period. These journals (three by Edward, three by Richard, and one by Benjamin) cover Frémont's fourth expedition, the Navajo expedition of 1849, and the Pope and Sitgreaves expeditions of 1851. Earlier editings of the fourth-expedition diaries can be found in Blanche C. Grant, *When Old Trails Were New: The Story of Taos* (New York, 1934), pp. 116–41, and in an unpublished master's thesis by Margaret A. Blythin at the University of California, Berkeley. These are now superseded by the inclusion of the Kern diaries in LeRoy R. and Ann W. Hafen, eds., *Frémont's Fourth Expedition: A Documentary Account of the Disaster of 1848-1849* (Glendale, Calif., 1960).

Besides the Fort Sutter Papers, the Huntington Library owns eight letters of Edward Kern (1846–52), three of Richard Kern (1849–53), and one of Benjamin Kern (1849), as well as a small group of letters addressed to both Edward and Richard.

Mary Kern's Album (including poems in the handwriting of Edward and Richard and a water color by Edward) is in the possession of Mrs. John Wolfe, Merion, Pennsylvania.

In the Newberry Library is a long letter of Richard Kern to Samuel George Morton, July 3, 1850, revealing in some detail the relationship between the Kerns and eastern scientists.

One letter of Richard Kern and two referring to the brothers, all from the New Mexico period, are in the John R. Bartlett Papers of the John Carter Brown Library, Providence, Rhode Island.

The National Archives contain Richard Kern's field notes on the Sitgreaves Expedition. Edward Kern's journal of August 17, 1845, to February 15, 1846, is in the possession of Mr. and Mrs. Fred Cron, Dingman's Ferry, Pennsylvania. This is apparently the manuscript prepared by Edward and then abridged for an appendix to James H. Simpson's *Report of Explorations across the Great Basin of the Territory of Utah* (Washington, D.C., 1876). Portions of the Cron copy appeared in *Life, 46* (April 6, 1959), 95–104. The Crons also own several Kern sketchbooks.

The main collections of John C. Frémont materials, such as those at the Bancroft Library; at the Southwest Museum, in Los Angeles; and in the National Archives (especially Selected Records Relating to Frémont, 1842–90, from the

General Accounting Office), contain no Kern writings, but they are all, of course, essential to his story. The papers appear in Donald Jackson and Mary Lee Spence, eds., *The Expeditions of John Charles Frémont,* 2 vols. and supplement (Urbana, Ill., 1970–73).

Aside from Frémont, probably the western associate whose writings help most in re-creating Edward Kern's life is Theodore Talbot. Talbot's letters, 1845–63, are in the Library of Congress and cover the third expedition, which the published Talbot journal does not. They have been edited by Robert V. Hine and Savoie Lottinville in *Soldier in the West* (Norman, Okla., 1972). The Charles Preuss diaries (1842–44, 1848–49) are also in the Library of Congress in the original German. They have been translated and edited by Erwin G. and Elisabeth K. Gudde in *Exploring with Frémont: The Private Diaries of Charles Preuss* (Norman, Okla., 1958). Likewise helpful is John F. McDermott's edition of the Alfred S. Waugh autobiography for 1845–46, *Travels in Search of the Elephant* (St. Louis, Mo., 1951). In the Scripps College Library, at Claremont, Calif., is the journal of Isaac Cooper (pseud., François des Montaignes) covering the first part of the Frémont third expedition. In different form it was published in the *St. Louis Western Journal and Civilian, 9-10* (1852–53) and *15* (1856), and has been edited by Nancy Mower and Don Russell in François des Montaignes, *The Plains* (Norman, Okla., 1972). The Thomas S. Martin manuscript "Narrative" and the George McKinstry Papers, both in the Bancroft Library, are important, as are the McKinstry Papers, in the State Library, Sacramento, Calif., and John A. Sutter's "Personal Reminiscences," in the Bancroft Library. In the Old Army Branch of the War Records Division of the National Archives will be found many reports and letters by James Simpson, John Parke, Lorenzo Sitgreaves, and John Pope relating to the Kerns in New Mexico. The John Gunnison correspondence and the Charles Pickett letters (both groups at the Huntington) are of lesser importance.

In the Ritch Collection at the Huntington Library are two items of interest on Kern: John Greiner's "Overawing the Indians" touches on Benjamin Kern's death, and a Charles Blumner warrant places Edward's legislative work and his salary.

The Bancroft and Huntington libraries contain small, nearly identical files by Helen Wolfe, "Some Kern Notes Written for Members of the Family from Data Collected over a Period of Years." The Bancroft material was assembled at the instigation of Herman A. Spindt, the pioneer student of the Kerns.

Secondary

There would be no reason to repeat here the bibliographies for such men and events as John C. Frémont, the California conquest, the Topographical Corps, and the early territorial period in New Mexico. All of them relate to the Kerns, but their bibliographies will be found in such standard works as Henry R. Wagner and Charles L. Camp, eds., *The Plains and the Rockies* (Columbus, Ohio, 1953); Allan Nevins, *Frémont: Pathmarker of the West* (New York, 1939); Ray Billington, *The Far Western Frontier, 1830-1860* (New York, 1956); or William Goetzmann, *Army Exploration in the American West, 1803-1863* (New Haven, Conn., 1959); and William Goetzmann, *Exploration and Empire* (New York, 1966).

Two pioneer studies have been made of Edward Kern: the first, Herman A. Spindt, "Notes on Life of Edward M. Kern," *Kern County Historical Society Fifth Annual Publication* (1939), pp. 4–20, was followed by a longer work by a student of Spindt's: William Joseph Heffernan, *Edward M. Kern: The Travels of an Artist-Explorer* (Bakersfield, Calif., 1953).

A helpful guide to the topographic explorations, in addition to William Goetzmann's books, mentioned above, is Gouverneur K. Warren, "Epitome of Warren's Memoir, 1800-1857," which appeared in the appendix to George M. Wheeler, *Report upon United States Geographical Surveys West of the One Hundredth Meridian* (Washington, D.C., 1889). The Kern mapping with Frémont, Simpson, Parke, Sitgreaves, and Pope is nicely handled in Carl I. Wheat, *Mapping the Transmississippi West, 1540-1861, 3* (San Francisco, 1959).

An analysis of Frémont's role in the California conquest is John A. Hawgood, "John C. Frémont and the Bear Flag Revolution: A Reappraisal," *University of Birmingham Historical Journal, 7* (1959), 80-100, which includes a shrewdly critical bibliographical essay. The good biography of Sutter, James Zollinger, *Sutter: The Man and His Empire* (New York, 1939), carries its bitter hostility toward Frémont over to Edward Kern, who is here described with no apparent justification as "a model of soldierly incompetence" and "a perfect military nincompoop" (p. 202). More sympathetic is Richard Dillon, *Fool's Gold: The Decline and Fall of Captain John Sutter of California* (New York, 1967). Kern's relations with Charles Pickett and some letters from Pickett to Kern can be found in Lawrence Clark Powell, *Philosopher Pickett* (Berkeley, Calif., 1942). Robert F. Heizer, "Walla Walla Indian Expeditions to the Sacramento Valley, 1844-1847," and John A. Hussey and George W. Ames, Jr., "California Preparations to Meet the Walla Walla Invasion, 1846," are detailed in their treatment of that episode in Kern's life; both appeared in the *California Historical Society Quarterly, 21* (1942), 1-21.

William Brandon's *The Men and the Mountain: Frémont's Fourth Expedition* (New York, 1955), not only is a work of literary power but contains a selective bibliography of the fourth expedition. Alpheus Favour, *Old Bill Williams: Mountain Man* (Chapel Hill, N.C., 1936; reprint, Norman, Okla., 1962), is the best biography of the close friend of the Kerns.

It can be supplemented by Chauncey P. Williams, *Lone Elk*, Old West Series, Nos. 6, 7), Denver, Colo., 1935–36), which includes many source extracts. Nolie Mumey, *John Williams Gunnison (1812-1853): The Last of the Western Explorers* (Denver, Colo., 1955), covers some excellent material on Richard Kern, reprinting letters and ephemeral newspaper clippings.

The basic work on western artists is Robert Taft, *Artists and Illustrators of the Old West, 1850-1900* (New York, 1953), based on Taft's articles in the *Kansas Historical Quarterly* from 1946 to 1952. The work, especially its footnotes, is a mine of information, but it makes no effort at artistic analysis. Taft's *Photography and the American Scene: A Social History, 1839-1889* (New York, 1938), does not deal with Kern but is helpful in assessing his photographic contribution, as is Beaumont Newhall, *History of Photography* (New York, 1949). Louise Rasmussen, "Artists of the Explorations Overland, 1840–1860," *Oregon Historical Quarterly, 43* (1942), 56–62, is no more analytical than Taft's *Artists.* The appendix, "The First Illustrators of the West," to Bernard De Voto, *Across the Wide Missouri* (Boston, 1947), does, however, deal critically with the earliest western artists: George Catlin, Karl Bodmer, and Alfred Jacob Miller. Later artists must be approached through their biographies or more general works, such as Wolfgang Born, *American Landscape Painting* (New Haven, Conn., 1948); or Fredcrick Sweet, *The Hudson River School and the Early American Landscape Tradition* (Chicago, 1945). An extremely valuable reference tool is the New-York Historical Society's *Dictionary of Artists in America, 1564-1860,* ed. G. C. Groce and D. H. Wallace (New Haven, Conn., 1957). See also Peter H. Hassrick, *The Way West: Art of Frontier America* (New York, 1977). The forthcoming book on Rocky Mountain artists by Peter H. Hassrick and Patricia Trenton (Norman, Okla., in press) is rich in methodological and stylistic analysis of the Kerns' work, including newly discovered items.

Edward Kern and the Pacific

Primary

For the two Pacific expeditions in which Kern was involved, by far the best collection of sources is in the Navy Branch of the National Archives. Journals of the Ringgold-Rodgers Expedition include those of William R. Baker (1853); F. H. Bierbower (1855); John M. Brooke (1853–54); Edwin O. Carnes (1853–55); Jonathan H. Carter (1853–56), plus Carter's private journal, which is particularly revealing; William Grier (1853–56); Henry Rolando (1853–54); Lewis M. Squires (1854–55); Henry K. Stevens (1853–55), one of the most literate of the journals; Frederic D. Stuart (1853–54), Ringgold's secretary, who included as an introduction to his journal a good statement of purposes and personnel; and Arthur Witzleben (1856). The Navy Branch collection also includes various reports of the commanders, Cadwalader Ringgold and John Rodgers. The Hydrographic Records are in the Navy Branch, but the charts of the expedition, many elaborately illustrated by Edward Kern, are in the Cartographic Branch. The Log of the *Vincennes* (1853–56) is in nine volumes in the Navy Branch; some of the volumes overlap when both rough and finished logs have been preserved, but the overlapping sections are not always identical.

Some of the more important records of the expedition have been edited by Allan B. Cole in *Yankee Surveyors in the Shogun's Seas: Records of the United States Surveying Expedition to the North Pacific Ocean, 1853–56* (Princeton, 1947). The extensive papers of the North Pacific Exploring Expedition, 1853–56, are held by the United States Naval Institute, Washington, D.C.

The large collection of John M. Brooke Papers in the possession of George M. Brooke, Jr., Lexington, Virginia, includes journals, letters, and reports. Brooke is editing some of the materials and has been most helpful to me in reporting Kern items. John M. Brooke published a short account, "Coasting in Japan: Voyage of the *Vincennes'* Launch from Simoda to Hakodadi," *U.S. Nautical Magazine and Naval Journal,* 5-6 (1856–57), 196–204, 278–87, 338–47, 411–22.

Two chatty eyewitness accounts from the ranks are Alexander W. Habersham, *My Last Cruise, or Where We Went and What We Saw* (Philadelphia, 1857), and Wilhelm Heine, *Die Expedition in die Seen von China, Japan und Ochotsk* (3 vols., Leipzig, 1858).

An extensive collection of letters, reports, and journals of John Rodgers is in the Naval Foundation Papers of the Library of Congress. The Library of Congress also holds the journals (1853–55) and papers of Frank A. Roe.

Cadwalader Ringgold published two short statements of his case against Perry in the removal proceedings: *Memorial of Commander Cadwalader Ringgold, United States Navy, to the Congress of the United States* (Washington, D.C., 1856) and *Defence of Commander Cadwalader Ringgold, before Court of Inquiry, No. 2* (Washington, D.C., 1857).

The Huntington Library owns a letter from William Jeffers to Richard Kern, April 28, 1852, which indicates the brothers' awakening interest in naval expeditions.

For a list of the thirty-nine scientific articles that grew out of the North Pacific Exploring Expedition, see Max Meisel, *A Bibliography of American Natural History: The Pioneer Century, 1769-1865* (3 vols., Brooklyn, N.Y., 1929), 3, 221–28.

For the 1858–60 expedition under John Brooke, the Navy Branch of the National Archives contains letters and reports, as well as the log of the *Fenimore Cooper* (1853–56, 1858–60). The Annual Reports of the Secretary of the Navy for the appropriate years invariably include reports by Brooke, as they did for the earlier expedition under Ringgold and Rodgers. Townsend Harris, *Complete Journal,* ed. Mario E. Cosenza (New York, 1930), provides helpful background, and the Townsend Harris Papers, in the College of the City of New York, contain references to the Brooke expedition. Several of the Japanese participants have published accounts: Joseph Heco, *Narrative of a Japanese,* ed. James Murdoch (Yokohama, n.d.); and a different and more selective translation of the same, Hikozo, *Hyoryu Ki: Floating on the Pacific Ocean* (Los Angeles, 1955); the Diary of Muragaki Awaji-no-kami in American-Japan Society, *First Japanese Embassy to the United States* (Tokyo, 1920); and Yukichi Fukuzawa, *Autobiography* (Tokyo, 1934; rev. ed., 1940, 1948).

Secondary

An excellent general background for the Pacific expeditions appears in A. Hunter Depree, *Science in the Federal Government: A History of Policies and Activities to 1940* (Cambridge, Massachusetts, 1957). F. V. Hayden, "United States Government Surveys," *American Journal of Science and Arts,* 2d ser., *34* (1862), 98–101, indicates the manner in which the Ringgold-Rodgers and Brooke reports were suspended by the Civil War. Charles O. Paullin, "Early Voyages of American Naval Vessels in the Orient," *United States Naval Institute Proceedings, 37* (1911), discusses the Ringgold-Rodgers and Brooke expeditions, pp. 407–17.

A short, specific treatment of the two expeditions is given by Allan Cole in "The Ringgold-Rodgers-Brooke Expedition to Japan and the North Pacific, 1853–1859," *Pacific Historical Review, 16* (1947), 152–62. The most detailed account in print of the northern parts of the Ringgold-Rodgers voyage is in Joseph E. Nourse, *American Explorations in the Ice Zones* (Boston, 1884), pp. 108–32. By far the best work on Brooke, based on the Brooke Papers mentioned above, is George M. Brooke, Jr., *John M. Brooke: Naval Scientist and Educator* (Charlottesville, N.C., 1980).

Although the Brooke expedition as such has received no exclusive treatment, its return on the *Kanrin Maru* is frequently discussed. These narratives include Allan B.

Cole, "Japan's First Embassy to the United States, 1860," *Pacific Northwest Quarterly, 32* (1941), 131–66; Chitoshi Yanaga, "The First Japanese Embassy to the United States," *Pacific Historical Review, 9* (1940), 113–38; and, earlier, Patterson DuBois, "The Great Japanese Embassy of 1860," *Proceedings of the American Philosophical Society, 49* (1910), 243–66.

Art Work

Original

Only three original paintings by Edward Kern in oil are known to be extant. Two of these are in the Museum of the United States Naval Academy, Annapolis: "View of the Coast of Japan, North Pacific Survey Expedition" and "Cutting Up a Whale on the West Coast of Kamchatka," reproduced in this book as Figs. 47 and 48. The latter was exhibited in a show, "American Processional," at the Corcoran Gallery of Art in Washington, D.C., in 1950 (the scene is not on Kamchatka, as labeled, but in Glazenap Harbor, to judge from a water color of the same subject and composition in Boston Museum of Fine Arts). The third is a portrait of Richard Kern in the National Collection of Fine Arts, Smithsonian Institution, Washington, D.C., reproduced here as Fig. 3.

Mrs. James F. McGarry, Jr., of Merion, Pennsylvania, owns an oil painting of a wagon in hill country, which, according to family tradition, is by Edward Kern. From the style, however, the ascription seems dubious.

The Boston Museum of Fine Arts houses eighty-one drawings and water colors executed by Edward Kern on the North Pacific Exploring Expedition, 1853–56. The Amon Carter Museum of Western Art, Fort Worth, Texas, now owns twenty-five water colors by Richard Kern executed between 1848 and 1852; two of these are reproduced as Figs. 54 and 55. David J. Weber is preparing a biography of Richard Kern for the Amon Carter Museum. The

Thomas Gilcrease Institute of American History and Art, Tulsa, Oklahoma, has twenty-four Edward Kern drawings and water colors of the Argentine, Paraguay, and Nicaragua. A small group of Kern Oriental water colors is in the possession of Mrs. Raoul Drapeau, Chelmsford, Massachusetts.

Among the original Kern sketches in the American West, the Academy of Natural Sciences of Philadelphia possesses sixty-nine drawings and water colors of New Mexico by Richard and Edward. Mr. and Mrs. Fred Cron, Dingman's Ferry, Pennsylvania, own seven Kern sketchbooks. The diaries in the Huntington Library contain occasional very sketchy drawings, and some of the Huntington letters, notably E. Kern to Mary Wolfe [late February or early March], 1849, are headed by elaborate art work. E. Kern to R. Kern, July 27, 1846, includes Edward's famous rough drawing of the Bear Flag Revolt, reproduced in *California in 1846: Described in Letters from Thomas O. Larkin, "The Farthest West," E. M. Kern, and "Justice"* (San Francisco, 1934).

The only other group of original Kern western drawings is in the Bushnell Collection of the Peabody Museum of Archaeology and Ethnology, Harvard University. It consists of three water colors by Edward and seven by Richard, plus four that are unidentified but are probably by one or both of the brothers. Some of the Bushnell Collection drawings are originals of later engravings or lithographs in Schoolcraft's *Indian Tribes.* Some were done in California, but most in New Mexico. Four Seth Eastman redrawings of Edward Kern sketches are in the J. J. Hill Reference Library, St. Paul, Minn.

Reproductions of Kern Art Work

The published accounts that included lithographs or engravings of Kern work appeared in roughly the following order: James H. Simpson, *Report and Map of the Route*

from Fort Smith, Arkansas, to Santa Fe, New Mexico, 31st Cong.,
1st Sess., Sen. Exec. Doc. 12 (Washington, D.C., 1850), two
lithographs from Richard's work; James H. Simpson, *Journal of a Military Reconnaissance, from Santa Fe, New Mexico,
to the Navajo Country . . . in 1849* (Philadelphia, 1852), private printing of the government document which had appeared two years earlier as a part of 31st Cong., 1st Sess.,
Sen. Exec. Doc. 64, seventy-five plates, some by Edward
and some by Richard, later edited by Frank McNitt, *Navaho Expedition: Journal of a Military Reconnaissance from Santa
Fe, New Mexico, to the Navaho Country* (Norman, Okla.,
1964); Lorenzo Sitgreaves, *Report on an Expedition Down
the Zuñi and Colorado Rivers,* 32d Cong., 2d Sess., Sen. Exec.
Doc. 59 (Washington, D.C., 1853), most of the twenty-three
nonscientific plates by Richard, some by Edward, and
many of the fifty-six scientific plates by Richard; Henry
R. Schoolcraft, *Historical and Statistical Information Respecting the History, Condition, and Prospects of the Indian Tribes
of the United States* (6 vols., Philadelphia, 1851–57), three
plates, plus at least three others not attributed but following drawings in the Bushnell Collection, by Richard in
vol. 4, and four plates and three small woodcut figures
by Edward in vol. 5; *Pacific Railroad Reports* (13 vols., Washington, D.C., 1855–60), *2,* twelve plates by Richard; Thomas
Jefferson Page, *La Plata, the Argentine Confederation, and
Paraguay* (New York, 1859), plates and figures by Edward.

Three Zuñi drawings by Richard Kern are included in
the Smithsonian Institution, *Handbook of North American
Indians: Southwest* (Washington, D.C., 1979), *9*:475. At least
two of the plates in John C. Frémont, *Memoirs of My Life*
(Chicago, 1886), are by Edward—those following pp. 88
and 441, to judge from the texts of pp. 483 and 484; many
others are likely Edward's, but there is no way of ascrib-
ing them for certain. It is possible that some of the cuts
from Habersham, *My Last Cruise,* especially opposite pp.
20, 194, 268, 296, and 356, are by Edward, but again there
is no sure way of knowing.

Index